Still on the Move
WARTBURG COLLEGE
A Sesquicentennial Celebration
1852-2002

WDG Publishing

Still on the Move
WARTBURG COLLEGE
1852-2002

Ronald Matthias

Frontispiece: Students in the Waverly arbor in 1912. Founders Hall now stands on this site.

Published by WDG Publishing

Still on the Move
Wartburg College
1852-2002

Creative Direction	Duane Wood
Design/Art Direction	Sam Otis
Production Management	Shari Boyle

Copyright © 2002 WDG Publishing

First published in the United States of America by
WDG Communications Inc.
3500 F Avenue NW
Post Office Box 9573
Cedar Rapids, Iowa 52409-9573
Telephone (319) 396-1401
Facsimile (319) 396-1647

Library of Congress Cataloging-in-Publication Data

Matthias, Ronald, 1933-
  Still on the move : Wartburg College, a sesquicentennial celebration,
1852-2002 / Ronald Matthias.
    p. cm.
  ISBN 0-9651620-6-0 (alk. paper)
  1. Wartburg College–History. I. Title: Wartburg College, a
sesquicentennial celebration, 1852-2002. II. Title.
  LD5721.W72 M38 2002
  378.777'34–dc21
                          2002152343

Printed in the United States of America

10 9 8 7 6 5 4 3 2 1

Acknowledgements

Thanks to everyone who shared with me their
understanding of the Wartburg story. And a
special thanks to those who have assisted in
"putting it all together":

Robert Gremmels, great-great grandson of
Georg Grossmann, for wise counsel in matters
editorial—and for suggesting the title,
Still on the Move.

Pamela Madden, Marianne Beck, and Robert
Wiederaenders, for guiding me through the
archival holdings of Wartburg College and
Wartburg Theological Seminary.

Linda Moeller, for encouragement and critiques,
and for sharing so generously the remarkable
resources of the Wartburg College
Communication and Marketing Office.

TABLE *of* CONTENTS

Foreword

"To everything there is a season, and a time to every purpose under Heaven." – *Ecclesiastes 3:1*

Pastor Wilhelm Löhe must have had this Bible passage from Ecclesiastes in mind some 150 years ago, when his love for a living Lutheran faith and education inspired his desire to serve German immigrants in America. For me, this verse so aptly characterizes the rich history of Wartburg College and continues to help us focus on the future.

Wartburg has weathered a variety of seasons since 1852, when Pastor Georg Grossmann and five brave students left Germany for Saginaw, Mich., to establish the school envisioned by Pastor Löhe. Throughout relocations and changing economic and educational climates, our leaders, faculty, and students have remained committed to the college's purpose: "To challenge and nurture students for lives of leadership and service as a spirited expression of their faith and learning."

Past successes have ideally positioned Wartburg College for progress and prominence. While we continue to focus passionately on the college's mission, it is our season and our time to take Wartburg to new levels of excellence. It is our time to build upon Wartburg's rock-solid values with a shared vision – not of a different Wartburg, but of an exceptional Wartburg, ready and better equipped to fulfill its mission as a college of the church in an increasingly interconnected world.

In this commemorative Sesquicentennial history, Dr. Ronald Matthias takes us through the Wartburg seasons of the past 150 years. His experiences as a student, faculty member, and vice president at Wartburg College give him a panoramic perspective on the college's complex history. His longtime association with Dr. Gerhard Ottersberg, Wartburg's first historian, enhances the narrative. Dr. Matthias' comprehensive research, attention to detail, and thoughtful writing about a place we all love make this work a fitting tribute to the Sesquicentennial celebration of a college "Still on the Move."

Jack R. Ohle
President
Wartburg College

CHAPTER ONE

The Finger of God

Wartburg College takes its name from one of the great castles of Germany. Established on a Thuringian mountaintop as a frontier fortress more than 900 years ago, the Wartburg was destined to become instead a center of German culture. For St. Elizabeth and Walter von der Vogelweide, it was a home. For Goethe, and Wagner, and Liszt, it was a place to seek inspiration. For Martin Luther, it was a place of refuge—and accomplishment. During his year at the Wartburg, Luther translated most of the New Testament into vernacular German, and in the process created a standard for the development of a uniform German written language. More recently, the castle has been transformed into a magnificent museum, and has become a destination of choice for European travelers. In 1999 it received UNESCO World Heritage designation.

Old Main in Clinton *(left)* served as a center of learning at Wartburg College for 40 years.

courtesy: Wartburg Theological Seminary

Wilhelm Löhe (1808-1872) His influence came to radiate throughout the Lutheran churches of nineteenth-century Germany and America.

Many of the centuries-old traditions of the Wartburg—culture, courage, continuity, change—live on in the life of Wartburg College. But

Die Wartburg von Süd-West

The Wartburg
Established on a Thuringian mountaintop as a frontier fortress more than 900 years ago, the Wartburg was destined to become instead a center of German culture.

despite its name, the college is not a direct descendent of the Wartburg. The origins of Wartburg College lie elsewhere: in the small Bavarian village of Neuendettelsau—and in the missionary efforts of its pastor, Wilhelm Löhe.

Despite spending most of his life as the shepherd of a poor, rural parish, Löhe's influence came to radiate throughout the Lutheran churches of nineteenth century Germany and America. His pastoral activities, his preaching, his writing, and his letters all testify to a deep Christian piety and a faith active in love. Löhe listened for God's call—and then responded. "I seek to serve," he said. And serve he did. The result was an incredible "legacy of care."

In Neuendettelsau, this legacy was expressed in Löhe's creation of a whole series of Lutheran charitable institutions: an orphanage, hospitals, asylums, schools, and a motherhouse for deaconesses. Thanks to Löhe's efforts and to the commitment of those who followed him, Neuendettelsau became and has remained ever since a remarkable center of Christian mission and ministry.

Early in his career, however, Löhe's interests in mission were focused less on Germany than on the New World. Large numbers of German immigrants—many of them Lutheran—were seeking new homes on the American frontier. Land was plentiful; Lutheran preachers and teachers were not. The prospects for increasing their numbers from traditional sources were totally unpromising.

For Löhe this was a call to service—and he responded with characteristic vigor. In Löhe's mind, what was needed was the preparation of men for service in the New World as "emergency" pastors and teachers. He decided to invite gifted young men who could not afford to get a higher education in Germany to undertake a period of "practical" training for ministry. Following completion of the training, they would be sent to serve in America. To those who complained that this involved a reduction in standards, Löhe responded with the argument of necessity. At first, he offered the training on a private basis, but within a few years established a seminary, first at Nürnberg, subsequently at Neuendettelsau.

Then Pastor Löhe came to me one day with the unforgettable words: "I still have no one whom I can send. The finger of God points to you." Who was I that I could defy God! My answer was: "Here am I, send me."

Georg Grossmann (left), writing in 1863 on his call to go to America

In the New World, Löhe's men at first offered their services to existing churches, such as the Ohio Synod. In 1847, however, Löhe took steps to encourage the formation of the Lutheran Church Missouri Synod, and then made a major contribution to its growth by providing for it a practical seminary at Fort Wayne, Indiana.

The youthful synod needed not only pastors but also teachers for its congregational schools. Once again Löhe responded. In 1852, he sent a young teacher, Georg Grossmann, and five students to Saginaw, Michigan, to begin a "seminary" for parish school teachers—the first of its kind in America. No one, of course, understood it at the time, but the little school created in Saginaw in 1852 was destined to become Wartburg College.

Saginaw had been at the center of Löhe's missionary interests for many years. During the 1840s he had assisted in the establishment of a series of German colonies in the Saginaw valley. Beginning with Frankenmuth in 1845, Löhe contemplated the creation of compact, worshipping German communities that might serve as models of

Christian living and as bases for missionary outreach, particularly to the Native Americans (in Löhe's words, "the heathen") who lived nearby. In addition, Löhe had hoped for some time to build in Saginaw a temporary shelter for newly arrived immigrants: a *Pilgerhaus*. By 1852, financial constraints caused him to conclude that the *Pilgerhaus* and a teachers seminary would need to be combined in a single building in Saginaw. Georg Grossmann was expected to take responsibility for both.

Interestingly, Grossmann was not Löhe's original choice to undertake this mission. A man named Hacker backed out at the last minute, and Löhe turned to Grossmann, who had recently arrived at Neuendettelsau. Grossmann was an experienced teacher; more recently he had been a theological candidate at Erlangen.

Grossmann set sail with his family and the five students in April 1852. They arrived in Saginaw mid-June and were warmly received by the resident Missouri Synod pastor. But when they asked to see the *Pilgerhaus*, they were shown an empty lot and a

Neuendettelsau

Thanks to Löhe's efforts and to the commitment of those who followed him, Neuendettelsau became and has remained ever since a remarkable center of Christian mission and ministry.

The Pilgerhaus
in Saginaw,
Michigan, became
the birthplace of
Wartburg College.

pile of lumber. So Grossmann rented an abandoned store building, complete with broken windows, and began instructing his students there on July 1, 1852. During the next several months, the students managed to combine learning with assistance in the construction of the *Pilgerhaus*. When it was finished in late autumn, the teachers seminary had a home.

But not for long. Within a few months, the relationship between Grossmann and the Missouri Synod, initially very cordial, began to sour. In part, it was a matter of theology. Löhe and the synod had come to disagree on certain Lutheran doctrinal matters. Grossmann stood with Löhe in the dispute, believing that the differences need not disturb Lutheran confessional unity and common mission. Missouri Synod leadership, on the other hand, was unwilling to tolerate any belief that was not fully in agreement with its official position. Before long, Grossmann found himself dealing with charges that he was a false teacher and that Löhe had forsaken the Lutheran Church.

Even more fundamental and disconcerting was the issue of control. The Missouri Synod

expected that the teachers seminary—and Grossmann as well—would stand under its jurisdiction. Löhe, however, insisted on keeping the school in his own hands. Similarly, Grossmann was unwilling as a pastor to affiliate with the synod (though he became a member of one of its congregations in Saginaw). For the Missourians this was intolerable. If Löhe and Grossmann would not submit, the teachers seminary must be closed, or go to another place where the synod had no congregations.

To the apparent surprise of synod leadership, Grossmann took up the challenge. He was not willing to submit, nor was he willing to close the school. He decided instead to take it elsewhere. Löhe was consulted and gave his approval. Pastor Johannes Deindörfer and Karl Gottlob Amman, friends and allies of Grossmann from the nearby Frankenhilf colony, traveled to Iowa in the summer of 1853 in search of a new location. Northwest of Strawberry Point in Clayton County they found an area that seemed to be a promising site for a German colony and the teachers seminary.

CHAPTER TWO

Many Places Quickly

Dubuque – Grossmann and Deindörfer and their families left Saginaw in September of 1853. They were accompanied by two students, by Amman and his family, and by a few adventurous souls from the Saginaw area who decided to seek new lives on the Iowa frontier. Traveling by boat, train, and wagon, and with few resources beyond their faith in "the helping hand of God" and their confidence in each other, this little band of twenty-two colonists arrived at Dubuque in early October 1853.

Dubuque was not their destination. But for the moment they could not go on. They were

Johannes Deindörfer *(left)* and **Karl Gottlob Amman** *(right)* found an area in Clayton County, Iowa, that seemed to be a promising site for a German colony and the teachers seminary.

literally penniless. Their last half-dollar had paid the ferryman who took them across the Mississippi River; proceeds from the sale of some assets in Michigan were not yet in hand. Grossmann made the rounds of Dubuque bankers, finally securing a substantial advance. This made it possible to pay their bills. More important, it enabled Deindörfer and Amman to proceed to Clayton County to begin laying the groundwork for a new colony they named St. Sebald.

Grossmann, however, did not go along. He was impressed with Dubuque and its potential; it seemed to offer many advantages for the development of his school. Within a matter of weeks, Grossmann had rented a house in Dubuque, welcomed a new group of students sent by Löhe, and reopened the teachers seminary.

The year went well; a second class graduated in 1854. Both Löhe and Grossmann, however, quickly came to the realization that the Michigan model would not work in Iowa. Deindörfer's dream of a substantial colonization effort at St. Sebald ran into the harsh reality of Löhe's inability to fund it. And Lutheran congregations still unborn were unlikely to need parish school teachers. Consequently, Löhe and Grossmann began to shape a new approach.

In addition to his teaching, Grossmann began gathering a Lutheran congregation in Dubuque and connected to it a parish school. Similarly, Deindörfer ministered to Germans who were already living in Clayton County. Clearly what was needed was more of the same: a sustained mission effort among German immigrants who in the early 1850s were flocking into Iowa on their own. Such an effort would require pastors. In its early stages at least, it would not require parish school teachers.

Events unfolded quickly in 1854. Löhe recommended to Grossmann the formation of a new Lutheran synod, and then took steps to double

the size of the prospective clergy roster by sending over two young men whom he had trained. On August 24, 1854, the four of them—Georg Grossmann, Johannes Deindörfer, Sigmund Fritschel, and Michael Schüller—met at St. Sebald to establish the German Evangelical Lutheran Synod of Iowa. With only four pastors and two congregations, prospects for the new synod were meager in the extreme. But the founders were confident that with the help of God they could find ways of responding to the mission needs and opportunities of the upper Mississippi valley.

None of this, of course, could happen without pastors. Some might continue to come from Neuendettelsau, but the synod clearly would need to develop its own. Grossmann, therefore, agreed to concentrate on theological education rather than teacher training. The implementation of this decision in 1854 marks the beginning of Wartburg Theological Seminary. It marks, however, neither the end of nor a break in the institutional continuity we have come to identify with Wartburg College. Teacher training may have been suspended for a time; but in its place came the beginnings of a different educational venture. Once again, the vision was Löhe's.

In urging the creation of the Iowa Synod, Löhe recognized that the training of pastors on an emergency basis would not be sufficient for the long run. Ideally, a theological seminary ought to provide education rather than training. This, in turn, meant admission of students who had completed a program of preparatory studies. So Löhe commissioned Sigmund Fritschel, one of the young men whom he sent to Iowa in 1854, to join

Sigmund Fritschel *(pictured)* and Michael Schüller were sent by Löhe in 1854 to help establish the German Evangelical Lutheran Synod of Iowa.

Grossmann in Dubuque and establish there a preparatory department (*Lateinschule*). This "Latin school" offered classical studies to teenage boys seeking admission to the seminary. The initial class consisted of three students: two from America and one from Germany.

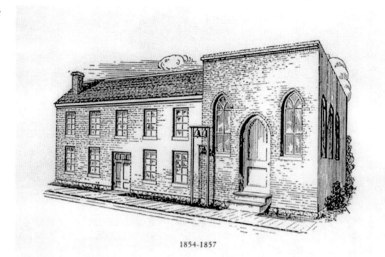

1854-1857

Löhe provided funds for the purchase of a building in Dubuque.

By the end of 1854, foundations for the three educational institutions that have come to bear the name Wartburg were in place. Grossmann's program of teacher education, which had begun in Saginaw in 1852, was suspended but not abandoned; eventually it became the centerpiece of Wartburg Normal College. The program of theological education that got under way in Dubuque in 1854 subsequently took the name Wartburg Theological Seminary. The little *Lateinschule*, established by Sigmund Fritschel—also in Dubuque, also in 1854—was destined to become Wartburg College.

Each institution bore the stamp of Wilhelm Löhe. Initially, Löhe provided nearly total financial support—including funds for the purchase of a building in Dubuque. Within a year or two, however, support from Neuendettelsau began to diminish—in part because Löhe believed that the Iowa Synod needed to become more self-reliant, in part because the view from Neuendettelsau was sometimes very different from that in Dubuque. Impatience on both sides escalated into mistrust; in late 1856 Grossmann journeyed to Neuendettelsau in an attempt to restore the relationship.

Reconciliation was effected, but it did not pay the bills. For several years during the mid-1850s, the seminary lurched from crisis to crisis. Students were few; attrition was high. Even so, the building was overcrowded. The fledgling synod agreed to assume ownership of the seminary, but could contribute virtually nothing to its support. Several times the school had to be closed down temporarily for lack of funds. Several times Grossmann faced the prospect of foreclosure by creditors. New loans, including a substantial one from a student (financial aid in reverse!), saved the day. But loans had the habit of requiring repayment.

The tiny staff of two teachers was cut in half when Sigmund Fritschel accepted a call to a parish with the understanding that he might be recalled when conditions improved. Until the arrival of Sigmund's brother Gottfried in 1857, Grossmann had to carry the full load of both theological and preparatory instruction. In addition, he continued to serve as pastor of St. John's congregation in Dubuque and as president of the Iowa Synod!

The seminary in Dubuque managed only a miserable existence and was often close to dissolution. Neuendettelsau provided support, but could not give enough. Congregations, still small and poor, showed little interest. Few of the early students had gifts for ministry and Christian earnestness.

Georg Grossmann (1866), recalling the early years in Dubuque

St. Sebald

Clearly things were not going well in Dubuque. What should be done? The answer came in a willingness to take a new look at Deindörfer's dream of combining the seminary with the settlement at St. Sebald in Clayton County. A rural setting promised the possibility of a self-sustaining community living mostly off the land. Not everyone was excited about the prospect of leaving Dubuque, but continuing financial adversity seemed to offer no alternative. Consequently, in early 1857 the Iowa Synod decided to buy some farmland at St. Sebald and to move the seminary there.

Sale of the Dubuque property was expected to provide the necessary funds. Had a sale been completed immediately, the real estate at St. Sebald might have been virtually debt-free. Instead the synod decided to hold the Dubuque property for a year to take advantage of booming real estate prices. This early attempt at financial creativity proved to be a disaster. The financial panic of 1857 destroyed the real estate market in Dubuque; the seminary property became almost worthless.

In the meantime the move to St. Sebald had been undertaken on the basis of borrowed funds. Everything was done quickly. A farm about two miles southwest of the St. Sebald church was acquired. Grossmann developed plans for a two-story frame structure, 32 x 48 feet in size, designed to house the entire enterprise. With the assistance of his theological students, he spent the summer and fall of 1857 erecting the new building. At the dedication on October 31, 1857, the seminary had a name: *Wartburg.* The new location was on high ground, and the view was magnificent, but it required a considerable stretch of imagination to compare it in any other way to the Wartburg in Germany. More important, perhaps, was the expectation that this new seminary, like the old castle, would breathe the spirit of Martin Luther.

Grossmann was in charge; initially he and Gottfried Fritschel did the teaching. Increasingly, however, Grossmann found it necessary to concentrate on his responsibilities as president of the Iowa Synod and as pastor at St. Sebald. Sigmund Fritschel was recalled; thereafter, he and his brother

St. Sebald

With the assistance of his theological students, Grossmann spent the summer and fall of 1857 erecting the new building. At the dedication on October 31, 1857, the seminary had a name: *Wartburg.*

Seminary students at St. Sebald, 1862-63: Graening, Prottengeier, Kaeding, F. Lutz, Seyler (*front row*); unknown, Jos. Meyer, F. Matter, Vogel, Rembold, Koehler (*back row*)

Gottfried not only did the teaching, but handled most administrative matters as well.

Wartburg at St. Sebald was both seminary and preparatory school. Though housed together and sharing the same faculty and even some courses, the two programs retained essentially separate identities. Students could be admitted to the preparatory program following elementary school and confirmation (usually about age 14). The curriculum, a truncated version of the German *Gymnasium*, placed heavy emphasis on classical languages–though instruction in English was also included. For more mature students, a shorter alternative was available. In either case, these studies were intended to prepare students for seminary. Within a few years, however, Wartburg was also encouraging the admission of students who did not plan to become pastors. Admittedly, not many young men responded to the opportunity.

Nevertheless, the preparatory program increasingly took on characteristics of a college– albeit for students much younger than college students today. By 1864, it was described as a *"Collegium"*; on several occasions the synod considered separating it from the seminary. But that would have required resources that simply were not available.

For the first few years at St. Sebald, Wartburg continued to live in imminent danger of financial ruin. Without a buyer for the Dubuque real estate, there was no way to retire the indebtedness that had been incurred in moving to the countryside. Once again, short-term borrowing bought some time, but by 1860 the situation was critical. Major loans were coming due; the meager resources of the Iowa Synod could not even begin to pay them off.

In desperation the synod sent Sigmund Fritschel to Europe to try to raise the necessary funds. Löhe was not in a position to provide much by way of assistance, but he did provide valuable introductions to prospective donors. Fritschel spent more than a year traveling throughout Europe in an exhausting fund-raising effort. His greatest success came among German communities of Russia–especially in the Baltic provinces. Returning to America in 1861, he brought with him enough money to keep the creditors at bay and the little seminary alive. In the process he established friendships that resulted

We knew little about coffee, tea, and other such items of luxury. We drank wheat coffee, had fresh meat only once a year when we butchered and salted our hogs, ate on tables and sat on benches which we made ourselves, and lived at the edge of a forest that looked over endless uncultivated prairie, isolated and separate from the world. Indeed, it was an unusual event if someone strayed to our Wartburg.

Sigmund Fritschel (1894), recalling life at St. Sebald

The college in Galena was never given a name. In Iowa Synod circles it was simply *das Collegium*. For English-speaking audiences it was the "German Evangelical College."

in a flow of sustaining funds to Wartburg for many years to come.

Given the beauty of the Clayton County countryside, life at St. Sebald was sometimes idyllic. But mostly it was very hard—and incredibly isolated. The isolation was partly geographic; to some degree it was self-inflicted. Students and faculty were committed to Löhe's vision of mission to German immigrants and to Native Americans. Their agenda did not include an interest in much of the world around them. Except for some complaints about inflationary prices, the Civil War and the monumental issues that surrounded it appear to have passed almost unnoticed at St. Sebald.

Even student numbers were largely unaffected by the war, remaining essentially stable at fifteen to twenty per year. Ordinarily about half of the enrollment was in the preparatory program, half in the seminary. Following the war, however, Wartburg's growth reflected the rapid development of the Iowa Synod. By 1867, thirty students were crammed into an increasingly inadequate facility at St. Sebald.

Galena

With prospects for even larger enrollments ahead, the synod decided not to add facilities at St. Sebald, but instead to separate the *Collegium* from the seminary. The seminary, under the continuing direction of the Fritschel brothers, would remain at St. Sebald, retaining the name Wartburg; the college was moved in 1868 to Galena, Illinois. Even though it now had separate institutional status, the college in Galena was never given a name. In Iowa Synod circles it was simply *das Collegium*. For English-speaking audiences it was the "German Evangelical College."

The move of the college from St. Sebald to Galena was the third move in fifteen years; it was the first in which the "pull" of new opportunity was stronger than the "push" of escape from overwhelming difficulties. The prophet of new possibilities in Galena was Johannes Klindworth, a local pastor who had a reputation for strong leadership in both the Iowa Synod and the Galena community. Klindworth proposed using a handsome brick building in downtown Galena for the synod's college. The structure had once housed a convent, but was now vacant and could be acquired at a bargain price. Klindworth argued his case persistently and persuasively. Despite some opposition from proponents of St. Sebald, the synod decided in 1868 to separate the college from the seminary and to move it to Galena.

Friedrich Lutz,
age 21, and Maria
Schulz on their
wedding day,
October 1863

Not surprisingly, Klindworth was placed in charge. He seems to have relished his new responsibilities; but since he was still pastor of the local congregation, he found time for only a little teaching and some fund-raising. Most day-to-day responsibilities—both instructional and administrative—were given over to Friedrich Lutz, a young pastor who a few years earlier had assisted Klindworth in the Galena parish. Lutz was immensely talented; as a graduate of both programs at St. Sebald, he understood the nascent Iowa Synod tradition in education.

The "German Evangelical College" at Galena was opened in the fall of 1868 with high expectations. The primary mission was still preparation of

students for seminary studies. However, there was hope that the urban setting of Galena would attract students with other interests as well—including even some non-Lutherans. The introductory announcement in the Galena *Gazette* indicated that the six-year course (once again modeled on the German *Gymnasium*) would prepare young men for university studies in "Philosophy, Law, Medicine, or Theology."

In another time and place, this combination of booster spirit and educational vision might have succeeded. It did not do so in Galena. The first year was somewhat promising; but the promise was never fulfilled. Before long, high hopes were replaced by yet another desperate search for survival. The litany of disappointments was familiar: small enrollments (ordinarily 15-20 students); inadequate facilities; high attrition; and, of course, not enough money. The six-year program was never fully implemented. Few students graduated. Even fewer young men from the Galena community were attracted to a school so thoroughly German in character. Klindworth, it turned out, had no enthusiasm for either the English language or for English-speaking students.

The Galena dream may have been an impossible dream. The educational focus of the Iowa Synod had not yet moved much beyond preparation of pastors; struggling congregations found it difficult to understand why they ought to support a second institution. Even with the strictest economy, the college found itself unable to live within its means. As debts piled up, the synod considered in 1871 the possibility of recombining the college with the seminary at St. Sebald—or of closing the college altogether. Each alternative was rejected on grounds that it promised to create as many problems as it solved. For the moment the college would continue in Galena.

For the immediate future, all grand plans for development and administration must be dropped. We may aim at the goal of becoming a seedbed of German science and culture, but conditions will have to determine how the goal can be attained sooner or later.

Georg Grossmann on prospects in 1871 for the college in Galena

Johannes Klindworth relished his leadership role at Galena, but found time for only a little teaching and some fund-raising.

Despite good intentions, the Iowa Synod continued to find the responsibility of supporting both a seminary and a college more than it could manage—especially in the midst of a great depression created by the financial panic of 1873. Neither institution was adequately funded, but each had to endure constant complaint about the way it spent what little it had. The problem was exacerbated when the seminary was moved in 1874 from St. Sebald to Mendota, Illinois. Financial arrangements for the undertaking reinforced long-held suspicions of Klindworth and Lutz that seminary always came before college, and that the Fritschel brothers had too much influence in synodical affairs. Before long suspicion and animosity escalated into open warfare between Galena and Mendota. Some of the battle was fought on theological turf; some of it involved each side accusing the other of financial mismanagement; some of it was an expression of fears that the college might be closed in Galena and moved to Mendota. But at the most fundamental level it was a struggle for power in the Iowa Synod.

Klindworth clearly wanted control. And control meant destroying the preeminence of Sigmund and Gottfried Fritschel in synodical affairs. Prospects were promising. A number of Iowa Synod pastors disagreed with the Fritschels on certain matters of doctrine; others shared Klindworth's resentment of their power and influence.

Following a few inconclusive skirmishes, the "Galena men," as they were called, sensed an opening at the 1875 synod convention in Madison, Wisconsin. Grossmann was ill and unable to preside. During debate concerning the synod's theological position, Klindworth and his allies launched an all-out attack on the Fritschels. The attack failed; the Iowa Synod adopted a theological statement drafted by Gottfried Fritschel. When the synod took up the matter of its institutions, it was Klindworth and Lutz who were thrown on the defensive by questions concerning their stewardship of college resources. Neither provided answers. Lutz left the convention early, taking the financial records of the college with him. To make matters worse, delegates discovered that Klindworth had talked of leading an exodus from the Iowa Synod, and of taking the college along. The convention had had enough. It quickly decided to close down Galena and to recombine the college with the seminary in Mendota. Both Lutz and Klindworth were suspended.

Klindworth was defiant. In a series of pamphlets, he defended his own conduct and continued the attack on the Fritschels. His shrill rhetoric was both offensive ("fraud," "liar," "seducer") and counterproductive; almost no one rallied to his cause. Expulsion from the synod followed; Klindworth quickly disappeared into obscurity. Lutz, on the other hand, immediately broke with Klindworth, clarified the college's finances, cooperated fully in

The college in Galena was a nest of discord and confusion. Even if the financial condition had been satisfactory, the synod could no longer permit it to exist.

Iowa Synod vice-president Johannes Deindörfer (1875) on the decision to close Galena

closing Galena, and a short time later was restored to good standing in the synod. He would be heard from again.

The failure of the Klindworth insurgency ended the Galena experiment. It also enabled the synod to abandon for the time being its failed efforts to maintain two separate educational institutions. The old model of St. Sebald—seminary and college in a single place—was resurrected one more time.

Mendota

Mendota, a small community of 5,000 located in north central Illinois, became home to Wartburg Seminary in 1874. The college was moved from Galena the following year, but in point of fact there was little to move: no faculty, few students, little equipment or library. In its new home the *Collegium* retained its identity, but operationally it was little more than an appendage of the seminary.

Located near the seminary building, this house was utilized as a dormitory and classroom building for college students in Mendota.

A nearby house provided the college students with both dormitory and classroom space; they ate their meals and attended daily worship at the seminary.

Who was in charge? No one associated with the college in Mendota ever claimed a presidential title such as *Director*. A series of young faculty members were identified as *Hausvater* or *Rector*. They provided general supervision, but clearly their roles were subordinate. Faculty members (including the Fritschels) functioned as the institutional "directorate." Even so, it is altogether probable that executive leadership was in the hands of Sigmund Fritschel. He directed the seminary; since the college functioned as a subordinate unit, his authority extended over it as well. John Fritschel, a son of Sigmund who both attended and taught at the college in Mendota, later identified his father as "president" during the Mendota years.

Galena had taught the dangers of a reach that exceeded the synod's grasp. So it is not surprising that a "hunker down" mentality prevailed in Mendota. Galena's six-year program was compressed

into four years. No longer was there an effort to recruit students from the larger community. Virtually every student was headed for the seminary; many were second generation sons of Iowa Synod parsonages. One class of six students included four Fritschels and a Grossmann.

More than a few of the students were uncommonly talented; the same was true of the faculty. Consequently the college in Mendota helped produce a whole generation of leadership for the Iowa Synod—and for its educational institutions as well. Four future presidents of Wartburg College—August Engelbrecht, John Fritschel, Otto Kraushaar, Friedrich Richter—spent a portion of their lives as members of the college community in Mendota.

Despite some obvious strengths, the college was able to do no more than hold its own. Total enrollment fluctuated between 15 and 25 students; funding and facilities were barely adequate; new initiatives were unthinkable. Next door at Wartburg Seminary, however, things were different.

Thanks to an influx of students from Germany, the pattern there was one of growth, resulting in a desperate need for additional space. Inevitably all eyes turned to the college and to the possibility of moving it elsewhere. If this could be done, the seminary would enjoy an instant addition to its physical plant.

Separation seemed feasible—perhaps even desirable. A few years earlier in 1879 the Iowa Synod had established a teachers seminary in Waverly, Iowa. Its building still was not fully utilized. Why not move the college from Mendota to Waverly and combine the two institutions? Despite some misgivings, the synod approved. After ten years in Mendota the college—now for the first time called Wartburg College—took up residence in Waverly. The year was 1885.

CHAPTER THREE

...And Not So Quickly

Clinton – The early years in Waverly were the best years the college had ever seen. Combination with the teachers seminary worked reasonably well; student numbers increased, and a second building, North Hall, was added in 1888. By the early 1890s even this was inadequate, and the synod began to consider adding yet another dormitory. The city of Waverly promised $3,000 in assistance, but before a decision could be made, a more dazzling offer came from Clinton, Iowa. Implicit in the Clinton proposal was the prospect—one more time—of separation. The teachers seminary would remain in Waverly; the college could be moved to a new campus in Clinton at no net cost to the synod.

At its core, the "Clinton Plan" was a land-development scheme hatched by well-meaning local boosters. They proposed that the synod buy a farm on the west edge of the city, reserve enough land for a spacious campus, subdivide the remainder into lots, and use the proceeds from lot sales to cover the cost of land acquisition and construction of college facilities. With Clinton growing rapidly, the numbers seemed to add up. Synodical leaders gave their blessing, and delegates to the 1893 synod convention made it official: Wartburg College would move to Clinton. Within a matter of months, land was purchased, ambitious plans

College students at Mendota in 1883: Herman Fritschel, C. Kleinlein, B. Fuehr, Naumann *(first row);* Lichte, Geo. Fritschel, P. Kluepfel, F. Loeb, John Reinsch *(second row);* **Aug.** Bartels, Jos. Meyer, E. Combe, Kiesel, Dietz *(third row);* Herman Bredow, Geo. Weng, P. Pichler, Jul. Prottengeier *(fourth row)*

Old Main in Clinton: A magnificent building, a staggering load of debt.

were drawn, and a magnificent brick building began to take shape.

Unfortunately a plan conceived in a moment of speculative enthusiasm had to be executed amidst the awful realities of financial fright. Implementation of the Clinton Plan was barely under way when boom times gave way to the great panic of 1893. Suddenly no one was interested in buying the Clinton lots; those who already had done so (including more than a few luckless Iowa Synod pastors) found themselves the owners of worthless real estate. To be sure the college had a new facility, but in every other sense the Clinton Plan was a disaster. The resulting debt load was

staggering; constituent anger festered for years. The Iowa Synod and Wartburg College could give thanks for many things; successful real estate ventures were not among them.

Once the commitment had been made, however, there was no turning back. Construction of the new campus and building continued; by the fall of 1894, Wartburg College in Clinton was up and running with an enrollment of 66 students. The location was new; the mission and program were not. Most members of the faculty were transplants from Waverly; most students were pre-seminarians. The ideals of the German *Gymnasium* continued to infuse the curriculum. A six-year program was

Otto Kraushaar served effectively as president from 1899-1907.

In the religion class we often get dumb jokes. Otherwise we have good teachers.

Friedrich Schoenbohm (1896), describing his first days as a student at Clinton

American students who were expected to spend their lives serving German-language Lutheran congregations.

Clinton's first president was Friedrich Richter, a pastor who had served for a time on the Mendota staff. In a sense, Richter never had a chance. Fallout from the shattered dreams of the "Clinton Plan" haunted his presidency. The financial problems seemed intractable; morale in the synod and on campus was depressingly low. Richter held on for five years; when he resigned in 1899, almost no one seemed to mind.

The presidency of Richter's successor, Otto Kraushaar (1899-1907), was a different story. Kraushaar, the first layman to serve as president, came up through the ranks of the faculty. He had a reputation for being a great teacher; as president he immediately demonstrated uncommon executive abilities as well.

Kraushaar placed the stamp of his leadership on every phase of college life. He understood that to be president is to be a fund-raiser. He retired the Clinton debt, developed the campus, added a

provided, with an additional year of preparatory studies available for students whose educational background was deficient. Students, still mostly German-speaking but largely American by birth, were admitted following their elementary school years—often at age 14. In American terms, the Wartburg program took students through both high school and college—and did so in six years. But it was not education American-style. It was a thoroughly German model designed for German-

The Gymnasium at Clinton was added during Kraushaar's presidency.

(left) O. Kuhlmann, A. Proehl, and W. Sodt occupy "the bark" at Clinton (1914).

(inset) Students pose on top of Old Main in Clinton.

(top) Wartburg students take a break during a work project.

(bottom) A typical Wartburg classroom (circa 1907) featured gas lights mounted on the ceiling.

gymnasium, and created scholarship and endowment funds. He understood that the college needed to grow. Taking personal responsibility for student recruitment, he doubled the size of the student body to 127. In these and other ways, the college clearly moved beyond survival. Perhaps the Clinton decision had not been a mistake after all.

For the moment, these kinds of operational successes were enough for the Iowa Synod. They were not enough for Otto Kraushaar. He saw what few of his contemporaries saw: the time had come for Wartburg College to shift from a German to an American model of education—one which would serve not only pre-seminarians, but young Americans, both men and women, as well.

Kraushaar's articulation of the case for curricular reform and coeducation was remarkably astute. The Iowa Synod, however, failed to embrace his vision. Mired in the parochial models of the past, synod leadership continued its insistence that Wartburg serve the church by preparing young men for the seminary. Young women need not even apply.

Had Kraushaar been given more time, he might have found ways to effect the transformation of

He deserves all of the high praise which Hamlet gives his father: "He was a man, take him for all in all, I shall not look upon his like again."

G. J. Neumann (1928), remembering Otto Kraushaar

Students relax on the Clinton campus in 1903. Despite Kraushaar's efforts, the Iowa Synod was not yet ready to open Wartburg to women or update its curriculum.

the college. But it was not to be. The ravages of Parkinson's disease forced him to relinquish the presidency in 1907 — an unspeakable tragedy not only for him and his family but for Wartburg College as well. Kraushaar's dream of a "first-class American college plan" would have to await the arrival of a new generation of leadership in both church and college.

The choice of John Fritschel to succeed Kraushaar in 1907 may have been an obvious one. He, too, was a veteran teacher, having served the college in Mendota, Waverly, and Clinton. As a son of Sigmund Fritschel, he brought to the presidency one of the great names and traditions of the Iowa Synod. The initial promise of his leadership, however, was never fulfilled. Whereas Kraushaar had embraced the future, Fritschel idolized the past. He found in it the "right spirit," which was "the principle thing in all sound education." In his view curricular change threatened the traditional mission of the college. Accreditation would open the door to interference by external agencies. Athletics encouraged students to waste their time. And so it went.

The inevitable result was an increasingly fractious faculty and a dispirited student body. To make matters worse, enrollment spiraled downward. Young men of the Iowa Synod were attending college in increasing numbers, but unless they were pre-theological students, they did not often come to Clinton. If they came, they seldom persevered to graduation. And if they tried to transfer, they often had trouble getting credit for work completed at Wartburg College.

In 1913 the college made a half-hearted effort to turn things around by finally abandoning the structure of the German *Gymnasium* and by reorganizing into a three-year academy (roughly equivalent to high school) and a four-year college. In

What I had in mind at the time [1920-21] was a career in engineering. Wartburg was about the worst choice I could have made.

Otto Kraushaar [son of President Kraushaar] (1988) on his year as a student at Clinton

an effort to increase student numbers, a scientific course for non-theological students was added. Not added were the resources, both faculty and financial, that might have given the experiment a fighting chance. The result was predictable. Enrollment continued to decline; by 1917 it was only half of what it had been during Kraushaar's

John Fritschel *(left)* served as president from 1907-1919. He struggled unsuccessfully to find a formula that would turn the school around.

Otto Proehl *(right)* succeeded Fritschel as president and quickly grasped the need for academic reform. By 1928, Wartburg was a coeducational college of the liberal arts.

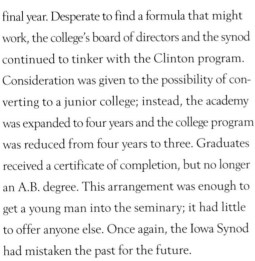

final year. Desperate to find a formula that might work, the college's board of directors and the synod continued to tinker with the Clinton program. Consideration was given to the possibility of converting to a junior college; instead, the academy was expanded to four years and the college program was reduced from four years to three. Graduates received a certificate of completion, but no longer an A.B. degree. This arrangement was enough to get a young man into the seminary; it had little to offer anyone else. Once again, the Iowa Synod had mistaken the past for the future.

With nothing going very well, a disheartened John Fritschel resigned the presidency in 1918 and resumed his career as a teacher of classical languages. His successor was Otto Proehl, a young pastor who brought to his new responsibilities not only a first-class mind and a deep commitment to "Christian education," but uncommon leadership abilities as well.

Proehl quickly grasped the need for academic reform. In 1920 the four-year college program and the A.B. degree were restored. But with college enrollment hovering around 50 students, more was clearly needed. By the mid-1920s, the college was prepared for radical curricular change. Under the leadership of Martin Wiederaenders, the faculty proposed that Wartburg College become a liberal arts college—complete with majors and electives—that it seek accreditation, that it offer a program in teacher education, and that it open its doors to women.

At stake was not only a change in educational mission, but the very survival of the college. Even the Iowa Synod was ready—finally—to abandon the ideals of the *Gymnasium* and to embrace a new order. Proehl skillfully managed the transformation; by 1928, most of the changes were in place. The dream of Otto Kraushaar had finally become reality: Wartburg College was a coeducational college of the liberal arts.

The "new" Wartburg got off to a promising start. Enrollment increased dramatically, more than doubling by 1930. Faculty positions were added; new buildings were planned; state accreditation was secured. All of this was encouraging—but it was not sufficient. The early 1930s found the college contending with powerful forces over which it had little control: the Great Depression, a new relationship with a new church, and the continuing presence of another Wartburg in Waverly.

The curriculum and the failure of the College to grow are cause and effect. A pre-theological college is doomed to failure . . . an unaccredited college, no matter what it may offer, is doomed to failure.

G. J. Neumann (1928) on the need for curricular reform at Clinton

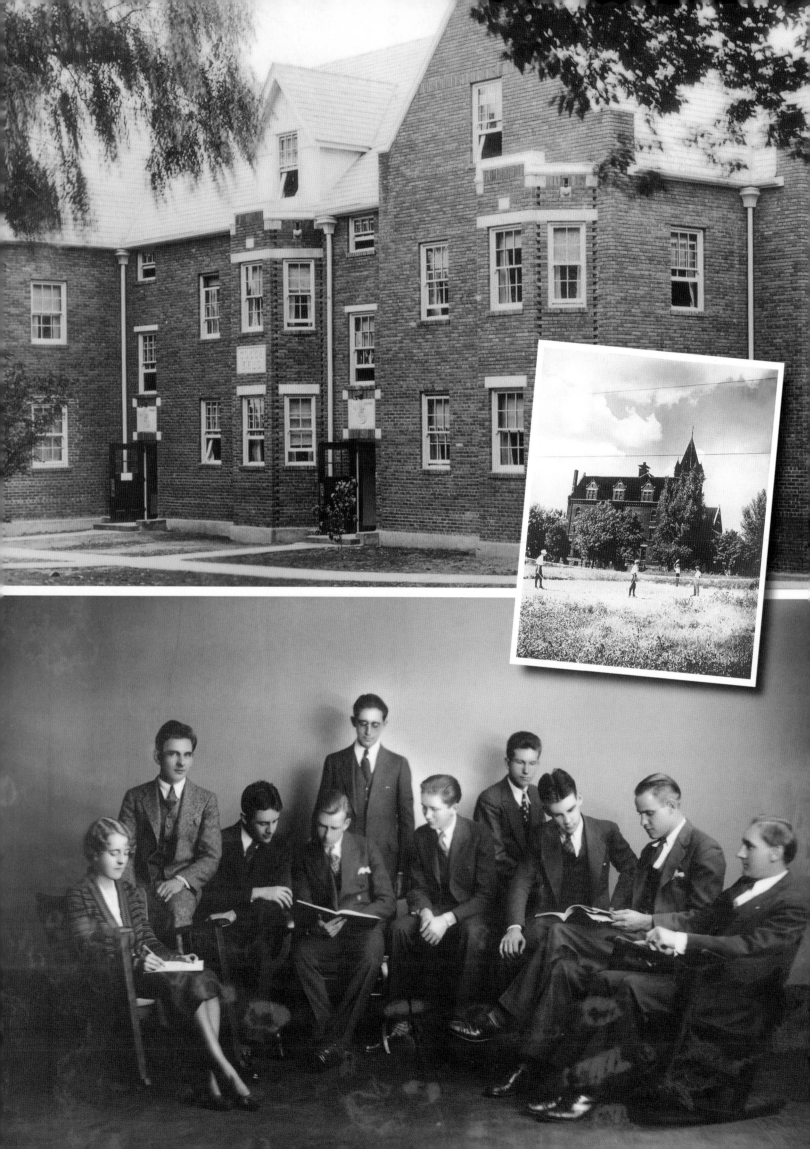

Waverly

Georg Grossmann came to Saginaw in 1852 to establish a "seminary" for parish school teachers. His move to Iowa and the establishment in 1854 of the Iowa Synod shifted educational priorities to the preparation of parish pastors. Given the meager resources of the new synod, teacher education had to be suspended for a time; but it was not forgotten. By the late 1870s, synod leadership was ready to give it another try; so was Georg Grossmann. In 1878, Grossmann—still serving as president of the synod—moved to Andrew, Iowa, gathered six students, and began to prepare them to become parish school teachers. The whole undertaking was clearly provisional. An underutilized synod orphanage provided space. Since Grossmann was already salaried, and since his assistant, F. Eichler, was paid by the orphanage, operational costs for the first year were only a few hundred dollars.

The Andrew experiment was both successful and brief. The following year (1879) the Iowa Synod decided to continue teacher training on a more substantial institutional basis. But where? Offers from two northeast Iowa communities, Andrew and Mitchell, were considered; however, a last-minute proposal trumped them both. Waverly, Iowa, offered $4,000 in building funds. In addition it claimed proximity to a large number of nearby Iowa Synod congregations, which could "supply our institute with food."

The Orphanage in Andrew, Iowa, doubled as a school for parish teachers.

The Waverly offer was accepted; the 1879-1880 school year began with Grossmann and Eichler providing instruction to thirteen students. After holding classes for a month in his home, Grossmann rented temporary space in a vacant hotel. Two square blocks of land in northwest Waverly were acquired ("far enough from the street to protect from the noise of traffic"), and in the fall of 1879 construction got under way on a three-story brick building. A year later it was ready for use.

Grossmann and his family occupied half of the first floor; kitchen and dining facilities were in the basement; classrooms and library were located on the first and second floors; the third floor was used initially as a dormitory. Pot-bellied stoves supplied the heat. Running water, electricity, and indoor plumbing made their appearance some years later.

(opposite page)

(top) **Cotta Haus** served as a dormitory for men.

(inset) Students play tennis on the Clinton campus.

(bottom) The 1931 Clinton student council

Georg Grossmann, still serving as president of the synod, moved to Andrew, Iowa, in 1878, gathered six students, and began to prepare them to become parish school teachers.

The size of "Old Main," as it came to be called, was mandated by the terms of the Waverly pledge. The building was more than adequate for an enrollment of twenty or so students; unfortunately, the cost (about $8,000) was twice as much as initially estimated. Grossmann covered some of the cost overrun out of his own pocket and assumed responsibility for raising the rest. It took several years of exhausting effort to erase the indebtedness; not until 1885 was the Iowa Synod willing to assume ownership of the Waverly campus.

For the synod there was another consideration. It had both a theological seminary and a college sharing inadequate facilities in Mendota, Illinois. The teachers seminary in Waverly, on the other hand, had space to spare. Consequently, in 1885 the Iowa Synod removed the college from Mendota and joined it to the teachers seminary in Waverly. The new combination took the name "Wartburg College."

Under the leadership of Georg Grossmann, things went well in Waverly. Blending teacher training with seminary preparation had its problems; nevertheless, the college thrived as never before. Moving student sleeping quarters from the third floor to the unheated attic of Old Main was one way of creating additional space; another was the addition of North Hall in 1888. Even more was needed. But instead of building in Waverly, the Iowa Synod became captivated by the prospect of something for nothing: an entirely new campus in Clinton, Iowa, at no net cost to the synod. It was the kind of offer that was difficult to refuse. So the decision was made. In 1894 Wartburg College, including most of its faculty and students, departed Waverly for the possibilities of new life in Clinton. Wartburg Teachers Seminary was left behind in Waverly.

It was left, however, with very little. Only nine students showed up for the opening of the fall term in 1894. Equally discouraging was the decision of an ailing Georg Grossmann to resign as *Director*. For the moment, Wartburg in Waverly had only one full-time teacher and a handful of students. Could it possibly survive?

The man called to succeed Grossmann was not altogether sure that it could. Friedrich Lutz regarded the teachers seminary as "completely crippled" by the departure of the college to Clinton. Nevertheless, believing that it was God's will, Lutz decided to take on the challenge and accept the call. In late 1894 he was installed as *Director* of Wartburg Teachers Seminary.

Lutz brought to his new position a creative mind and a wealth of experience, both in the parish and as a teacher. Twenty years earlier he had been the mainstay of the college in Galena; more recently, he had spent three years (1885-1888) as a member of the Wartburg College faculty in Waverly. His call to leadership in 1894 was neither the first nor the last in a long and distinguished career.

The challenge in Waverly was enormous. Not only had the college departed for Clinton; the historic mission of training parish school teachers was beginning to show signs of obsolescence. By the mid-1890s, parochial education everywhere was giving way to public education; most Iowa Synod congregations were finding it possible to manage without full-time teachers. Was there any reason any longer to keep alive a synodical seminary to train teachers? Probably not—unless somehow it could be transformed.

Transformation is precisely what Friedrich Lutz and his faculty colleague, August Engelbrecht, had in mind. They knew the Waverly area well and were convinced that adding some new programs with an American rather than German flavor would attract local students—and perhaps some from a distance as well. In part it was a matter of survival. But it was more than that. In the past, Wartburg Teachers Seminary had focused on the needs of the Iowa Synod. Henceforth, it would center its attention on the interests and needs of students. Lutz was able to

Friedrich Lutz succeeded Grossmann as the Director of Wartburg in 1894, and ushered in an era of dramatic change and growth.

The chief object has been to make work as thoroughly practical as possible. . . . Nothing, on the other hand, has been omitted of what is considered essential in the mental equipment of an efficient man, an intelligent citizen, and a true Christian.

Wartburg Academy catalog (1903)

Sunday afternoon on the Wartburg campus, 1909: Schauer, unknown, Moesenthin, Schafer, Meyne, Vorthmann, Voigt, Sandrock *(top row)*; Timmcke, Burrack, Ackermann, unknown, Deguisne, Heist, Gathmann, Lenz, Engelbrecht, Hankammer, Brokering *(bottom row)*

sell his vision to synod leadership; as a result, he could claim a mandate for change that was never available to his contemporaries in Clinton.

And the changes came: evening classes, a winter program designed to attract young farmers, an "Academy" offering elementary and business classes in the English language. Gradually, the Academy developed into a true academy: a four-year program on the high school level. Elementary education was organized into a "preparatory" program offering seventh and eighth grade courses. Business courses were combined into a Commercial Department; a Music Department was created to offer piano, organ, and instrumental lessons to both residential and Waverly-area students.

This educational potpourri with its distinctly American flavor appealed not only to young men but to young women as well. In 1896, more than a quarter-century before coeducation arrived in Clinton, Wartburg Teachers Seminary began accepting women students into several programs. And in 1907 the Iowa Synod agreed to the admission of women into teacher training. As

the emphasis of that program shifted toward preparation of students for teaching in public elementary schools, the enrollment of women increased dramatically. Within a few short years Wartburg in Waverly was thoroughly coeducational.

One program, however, remained a male preserve. In 1896 Lutz secured the transfer of the synod's "proseminary" from Wartburg Seminary in Dubuque to Waverly. This program, which had roots going all the way back to Löhe's training of "emergency" pastors, offered older-than-usual students the opportunity to undertake a two-year practical course (rather than the six-year classical course at Clinton) as preparation for theological study. The arrival on the Waverly campus of proseminary students not only swelled the enrollment; it added diversity in age to a mostly teenage student body. More important, it sowed seeds of competition between Waverly and Clinton. Henceforth, both institutions were in the business—albeit in very different ways—of preparing students for theological study in Dubuque.

Here in Waverly you can entrust your children with good conscience, even your daughters.

Director August Engelbrecht (1915) in an appeal for Lutheran students

A women's dormitory was available for the first time in 1910. It was, however, a rented facility, used until the completion of Wartburg Hall in 1913.

WE'RE FROM WAVERLY IA. A GOOD TOWN

WARTBURG ORCHESTRA
1000 MILE TOUR WAVERLY, IA.

(top) Students enjoy Outfly at Riverside Park.

(lower left) In good weather, classes were occasionally held outside. This class met where Founders Hall now stands.

(inset) The Waverly Orchestra traveled in style in the 1920s.

(lower right) Early tree huggers populate the campus, circa 1920.

Down the road this would mean trouble. But in the short run, it added one more string to Lutz's bow. The institution he bequeathed to his successor in 1905 scarcely resembled the teachers seminary he had inherited a decade earlier. Wartburg in Waverly had become a comprehensive school, offering a variety of mostly pre-collegiate programs to men and women, young and old, both residential and non-residential. Student enrollment was up—substantially. Furthermore, in contrast to Clinton, Waverly had demonstrated a willingness to embrace American patterns of education. For the moment, this meant a stronger commitment to opportunity than to excellence. The future would demand more than this. But at least the school was headed into that future.

Lutz's resignation in 1905 led to the election of Gerhard Bergstraesser, pastor of a large rural congregation near Waverly. Like Lutz, Bergstraesser seems to have been reluctant to accept the call; unlike Lutz, however, he never developed an enthusiasm for new possibilities. His focus was on the familiar—on maintenance rather than innovation. After four largely uneventful years, Bergstraesser decided to return to the parish.

And once again, some Iowa Synod leaders were ready to raise questions about the viability of their school in Waverly. The Bergstraesser years had witnessed a decline in student numbers. Further decline was anticipated as a result of decisions by western districts of the Iowa Synod to open academies in Sterling, Nebraska, and Eureka, South Dakota. According to a synodical official, the chief task of the next *Director* of Wartburg in Waverly would be to dig its grave.

That next *Director* was August Engelbrecht. Elected in 1909, he was determined to be a builder rather than a gravedigger. Like John Fritschel, his

counterpart in Clinton, Engelbrecht emerged from the ranks of the faculty. Like Otto Kraushaar, he was a layman. For nearly two decades he had been a leader—not only on campus, but in the Iowa Synod and in the Waverly community as well. He knew the school; he knew the constituency; he knew American education—and he knew what needed to be done.

August Engelbrecht, president from 1909 to 1933, was responsible for transforming a school into a college.

During the course of his quarter-century (1909-1933) presidency—the longest in Wartburg history—Engelbrecht transformed a school into a college. Along the way came some new community-based programs, such as agriculture and manual training—neither of which was very successful. More promising—and significant—was the addition in 1914 of a program in home economics "to fit young women for the responsibilities of intelligent housekeeping and home making." Director of the program was Henriette Pribnow, the first woman to hold a faculty position in an educational institution of the Iowa Synod. Offerings in home economics were supplemented in 1920 with the introduction of a required course in "Mothercraft" for all female students in the academy.

Engelbrecht was an enthusiast for coeducation, in part because he understood its potential for increasing student numbers. His commitment to quality ran even deeper. Wartburg Teachers Seminary and Academy (as it came to be called) had a generous mix of programs: teacher education, proseminary, academy, preparatory, commercial, music. But as yet none of them was academically strong. And each was functioning in an increasingly competitive environment. It was time—even past time—to undertake a quest for quality.

Engelbrecht had an eye for faculty talent, and was able to assemble an outstanding team that included three future college/seminary presidents (Edward Braulick, Henry Arnold, Julius Bodensieck). The addition in 1917 of a Ph.D. (Theodor Geissendoerfer) enabled Waverly to claim a bit of academic distinction that Clinton could not match.

Quality also meant curricular change. Engelbrecht beefed up the program of the academy, making it solidly competitive with area high schools. As a result, the State Board of Education accredited the academy in 1915, thereby making its graduates eligible for admission to state universities without passing an entrance examination. Accreditation of the academy by the North Central Association followed a decade later (1926)—the first such recognition for any institution of the Iowa Synod.

In the meantime, the teacher education program was strengthened, first by adding a fourth year, later by elevating the curriculum to the level of a junior college. As a result, it became feasible in 1920 to give the school a new name: Wartburg Normal College. Despite the name, it began attracting students interested in a liberal arts curriculum and by 1927 had received state accreditation as a junior college. This was great news for Waverly. Clinton, on the other hand,

Resolved, that Director Engelbrecht receive the sum of $150.00 as reimbursement for the numerous uncharged business trips . . . made in his own automobile. The Board feels that the rather alarming wheeze and the premature decrepitude of his Ford are largely due to the mileage covered by the machine in the interest of the school.

Minutes of the Wartburg Normal College Board of Directors (1929)

The addition in 1914 of a program in home economics was intended "to fit young women for the responsibilities of intelligent house-keeping and home making."

Grossmann Hall

(now Founders Hall) was built after World War I to accommodate growing enrollment.

grew increasingly nervous over the emergence of its sister institution as a collegiate competitor.

The growth in quality was matched by a growth in student numbers. At the beginning of Engelbrecht's presidency, enrollment stood at 84. It rose steadily for fifteen years, reaching 262 in 1924. Admittedly, these totals included many elementary-age students taking music lessons; nevertheless, all of the programs demonstrated a capacity to grow. Not surprisingly, this growth placed a severe strain on college facilities. In fact, without the construction of new facilities, it could not have happened.

Engelbrecht was a builder. And he was a master at convincing the synod to fund facility needs on the Waverly campus. First came a renovation of Old Main. In 1912 North Hall was doubled in size, thereby permitting the attic of Old Main to be retired forever as a men's dormitory. Women

students were at first housed in rented quarters, but in 1913 they were able to move into just-completed Wartburg Hall. Following World War I, a gymnasium and Grossmann Hall, a residence for men, were dedicated. Along the way, several wooden structures were built or acquired—including a prefabricated building, "The Portable," erected in 1921 between North Hall and Grossmann Hall to serve for a few years as a classroom annex. Engelbrecht's efforts to develop the campus culminated in the construction of Luther Hall in 1925-26. Designed to house administrative offices, classrooms, and the library, it came to be regarded as the finest academic building in the Iowa Synod—and, during the 1930s, in the American Lutheran Church as well.

Despite all these successes, it was apparent by the late 1920s that Wartburg Normal College faced an uncertain future. The Lutz-Engelbrecht

The reference books on Zoology and Botany are filled with evolution.

Report of the synod visiting committee to Wartburg Normal College (1926)

North Hall

(top) was doubled in size, allowing the attic of Old Main to be retired as a men's dormitory.

The extension *(bottom)* included a new dining room for men.

[Each room is] provided with two disappearing beds, which during the day are folded into the wall openings, which are ventilated through a connected system that reaches every room in the building and communicates with the outside.

From a college brochure (1922) describing special features in Grossmann Hall

in the music and commercial departments was slipping. And the Iowa Synod no longer had much need for a proseminary as a "practical" alternative to the "classical" preparation of pre-seminary students at its college in Clinton.

If Wartburg Normal were to have a future, it would have to develop as a two-year—and perhaps eventually a four-year—college. Unfortunately, prospects for that kind of future ran headlong into efforts of Wartburg College in Clinton to become a "standard" liberal arts college. In adding a program in teacher education and in admitting women students, Clinton was seeking not only to secure its own future. It was also attempting to beat out a competitor within the Iowa Synod. For years Clinton had viewed with alarm the development of a coeducational junior college in Waverly. Now it was ready to challenge Waverly by preempting its future. In the words of a Clinton faculty member, "Waverly must die." Waverly, quite understandably, had other ideas.

formula of building a limited collegiate program on a base of elementary/secondary offerings was beginning to show signs of obsolescence. By 1925 the preparatory (junior high) program was dead; despite North Central accreditation, the days of the academy clearly were numbered. Enrollment

CHAPTER FOUR

A Passion for Place

The decision of 1893 to divide Wartburg College—and to send most of it to Clinton—proved to be one of the great tragedies in the history of the college. Clinton, of course, was not the problem. It was an attractive community, and the campus there was magnificently situated.

The problem was the separation into two Wartburgs—neither of which could thrive in the presence of the other—neither of which was adequately supported—neither of which could develop a sense of permanence and place. And this was true despite some gifted leadership in both Clinton and Waverly.

The half-century during which two Wartburgs existed was a half-century of missed opportunities, of dead ends, of endless maneuvering for advantage. By the late 1920s, with the two colleges growing more and more alike, the question for the Iowa Synod was obvious: Why continue to maintain two colleges in eastern Iowa? Why not recombine them once again?

The case for recombination was strong. It would eliminate duplication, concentrate financial resources, and substitute one strong college for two struggling ones. The difficulty, of course, was that this involved choosing a winner and a loser. Presidents, faculties, and alumni from both Clinton

Wartburg Hall *(left)* was dedicated in 1913 to serve women students in Waverly.

Take me and try me,
Making a man of me.
But, fate, be not cruel
And send me to
Waverly.

Found on a Clinton classroom chalkboard (1929)

"Facts" argued for consolidation in Waverly. The faculty of Clinton prepared "Light on 'Facts'" as a rebuttal.

got nowhere. And so it was decided not to decide. For the time being, both Clinton and Waverly would continue as they were and where they were. If anything were to be done, it would have to be done at some future time by the American Lutheran Church (ALC), created in 1930 by the merger of the Iowa, Ohio, Texas, and Buffalo synods.

In the new church, the "college problem" in the Midwest became vastly more complicated. The Iowa Synod had operated three colleges in the area: Wartburg in Clinton, Wartburg in Waverly, and Eureka in South Dakota. The Ohio Synod brought into the merged church two others: Hebron in Nebraska and St. Paul-Luther in Minnesota. Did the American Lutheran Church really need five colleges in the Midwest?

There was no time to consider the question on its merits. As shadows of the Great Depression spread over the land, the new church quickly found itself desperately short of funds. So did the colleges, each of which was highly dependent upon an annual subsidy from the church. As the subsidy shriveled, and as more and more students found it impossible to pay their bills, the Waverly board in 1931 described itself as "fatigued and depressed" over the realities of a budget that was "maimed and mutilated . . . beyond recognition." Deficit spending was not an option; the church decided to mandate a "pay-as-you-go" policy for its institutions. All operational expenses were to be

and Waverly were determined that *their* Wartburg should survive. Waverly, with a clear advantage in terms of buildings, supported consolidation—provided, of course, that it be implemented in Waverly. Clinton partisans, recognizing the inadequacy of their facilities, argued instead for a new kind of division: a four-year college in Clinton; an academy and a few vocational programs at Waverly. When a group of Waverly enthusiasts published a pamphlet titled "Facts" for distribution to synod convention delegates in 1929, President Proehl complained that Clinton had once again become the victim of "false and malicious reports," "unchristian tactics," and a "lack of self-respecting cooperation." It was time to remove from Waverly the "unnatural ambition that forgets duty, honesty, and humility." The Clinton faculty promptly responded to "Facts" with a widely distributed pamphlet of its own: "Light on 'Facts'."

The controversy generated more heat than light, more anger than understanding. Efforts by the Iowa Synod in 1928 and 1929 to find a solution

If the people now conducting our school in Waverly . . . have lost faith in Christian education on the middle level, then we must ask synod to put in an entirely new crew that will have the mind and the courage and the joy to do that serious work for us that needs to be done in training Lutheran artisans, accountants, government clerks, and that vast array of middle level of professionals.

Clinton president Otto Proehl (1929) on the mission of Wartburg Normal College

paid in full; faculty and staff would receive pro-rata salary payments out of remaining funds. This arrangement insured balanced financial statements, but requiring that faculty and staff bear the full burden of substantive deficits seemed to many both dishonest and unjust. The most that could be said for the policy was that it was a desperate response to a desperate situation.

By 1932 it was difficult to argue any longer that the church should continue to support five colleges in the Midwest. The question that followed, of course, was the familiar one. How and where could consolidation best be effected?

This time, things seemed to fall into place. Hebron appeared to be holding its own; St. Paul-Luther was struggling; Eureka was barely alive. Wartburg College in Clinton was growing; Wartburg Normal in Waverly was not. When enrollment at Wartburg Normal fell by more than a third in the fall of 1932, its chances for survival seemed bleak—even to its champions.

Acting upon recommendations from its Board of Education, the American Lutheran Church, meeting in 1932 in Fond du Lac, Wisconsin, voted to undertake a consolidation that would reduce the number of midwestern colleges from five to three. Hebron was to continue; Eureka and St. Paul-Luther were to merge in St. Paul; the liberal arts and teacher education programs of Waverly and Clinton would be combined—in Clinton. Other Waverly programs, including the academy, were discontinued.

The decisions regarding location, however, were specifically provisional rather than final. In its action, the church mandated that the Board of Christian Higher Education (as it now was called) develop a plan for "the permanent location of a four-year college in the middle west." The meaning seemed clear. The church was looking toward a single college in the Midwest; the permanent location might or might not be Clinton.

While some church leaders were interested in an

> Waverly has splendid building facilities for the merger. All other argument favors a merger at Clinton.
>
> *From the report of the Board of Education to the ALC convention (1932)*

Clinton faculty, staff, and spouses (1930-31), including: President Otto Proehl *(front row far left)*, John Fritschel *(front row fourth from right)*, Martin Wiederaenders *(second row far left)*, and G.J. Neumann *(fourth row third from right)*

Classrooms in Waverly and Eureka sat empty after the 1932 decision to consolidate ALC midwestern colleges.

[President Proehl] said: "Do you blame me for fighting for my school?" I answered, "Not for the fighting for your school, but for the way in which you did it."

August Engelbrecht on a meeting with Otto Proehl following the 1932 merger decision

entirely new location (perhaps Omaha), funding prospects for this kind of undertaking were absolutely nil. Clinton partisans consequently found it easy to believe that the church would have no alternative but to keep its college in Clinton. After all, both Waverly and Eureka were under sentence of death. St. Paul-Luther and Hebron were still alive, but neither could ever hope to generate much enthusiasm in a Midwest filled with congregations of the former Iowa Synod. The battle was over; the future lay with Clinton. Or so it seemed.

The Wartburg community in Waverly handled the church's doomsday verdict with considerable grace. Despite the fact that it meant for him an end to more than forty years of association with the college, President Engelbrecht encouraged everyone to "work on faithfully," and to "do our duty." An editorial in the student *Wartburg Echo* recognized that the church had been required to choose between "one Wartburg and no Wartburg," and called upon alumni to "rally

around the New Wartburg" in Clinton. The closing words were astonishing: "In the spirit of sacrifice we are ready to serve the Church by continuing our work at the merged school."

Waverly partisans wisely avoided any criticism of the church; but they were not at all averse to expressions of bitterness toward Clinton. President Engelbrecht explained to his board that the dramatic decrease in enrollment in 1932 had been the result of a "ruthless campaign" of "unfair propaganda waged by Clinton against Waverly." At its final meeting, the Wartburg Normal board of directors seconded Engelbrecht's views by describing Clinton's behavior as "unLutheran," and by complaining that pro-Clinton delegates to the 1932 church convention had slandered Waverly by calling it a "hick town," and a "town in a cornfield." But after thoroughly venting its frustration, the board resigned itself to the inevitable: "There is nothing more to do, but to adjourn."

It will be necessary for us to break up our family life because there is no money to move our furniture to Clinton. Here in Waverly we did not even receive our salary for December 1932 so far.

Faculty member John Hiltner (1933) on the move from Waverly to Clinton

The Clinton/Waverly merger turned out to be not much of a merger at all. Only three Waverly faculty members (A. W. Swensen, Gerhard Ottersberg, and John Hiltner) were offered positions in Clinton; only three Wartburg Normal students transferred to Wartburg College in the fall of 1933. (An even larger number transferred to Luther College in Decorah!) Wartburg in Waverly was closed, not merged; the campus community was scattered to the winds. All that was left were vacant buildings—and memories.

And a measure of hope. President Engelbrecht, who was named custodian of the Waverly campus pending its ultimate disposal, continued to have faith that somehow Wartburg might return to Waverly. So did Waverly community leaders and a host of friends in northeast Iowa. They had some reasons for encouragement. Church officials immediately decided not to put the campus up for sale or to remove the contents of its buildings—just in case they might be needed again sometime.

Furthermore, while Clinton had possession of the college, its control was specifically provisional, pending a decision on a permanent location. Facilities on the spacious Clinton campus were unquestionably inadequate; it had, for example, no residence hall for women students. New construction was mandatory at Clinton; it would not be required if the college returned to Waverly.

In 1933 Waverly partisans undertook an attempt to convince the districts of the church to support the immediate creation of a single midwestern ALC college—presumably in Waverly. Except in Iowa, the effort garnered little support. But the "Waverly men," as they came to be called, did succeed in convincing the American Lutheran Church to hold its 1934 convention in Waverly. From the church's point of view, Waverly, with its empty college buildings and central location, was an inexpensive place to meet. From Waverly's point of view, hosting the convention was an opportunity to show off its buildings and to

Luther Hall, built in 1925-26, stood empty with the rest of the Waverly campus after the 1933 consolidation in Clinton.

convince delegates that Waverly was "one of the most modern of the smaller cities of Iowa." However modern, it was scarcely a neutral site.

During the spring and summer of 1934, the Waverly community was enlisted in an effort to prepare special hospitality for ALC convention delegates. Women of St. Paul's Lutheran congregation not only cleaned the buildings; they decorated each dormitory room as well. A volunteer taxi service was created; Boy Scouts were recruited to serve as convention couriers. Delegates were invited to travel via Dubuque or Clinton so that they might compare the facilities of Wartburg Seminary or Wartburg College with the ones they would experience in Waverly.

In Clinton, Waverly's efforts to reclaim the college were viewed as more of an irritation than a threat—especially after the Board for Christian Higher Education in early 1934 decided to recommend to the church continuation of Wartburg College at Clinton. In the words of one Clinton faculty member, "That removed the worry here. . . . [We] were not prepared for any reopening of the questions."

When the ALC general convention convened in October, Clinton's misplaced confidence was shattered by one devastating development after another. The Board for Christian Higher Education reported that it had changed its mind and was now prepared to recommend closing the campuses in Clinton and St. Paul, and reopening in Waverly. The floor committee on higher education (seemingly "packed" in Waverly's favor) also recommended a return to Waverly. During the deliberations, C. C. Hein, president of the church, launched from the chair a personal attack on Clinton's President Otto Proehl, accusing him of having misled the church two years earlier at Fond du Lac. Pro-Clinton participants were stunned as the convention moved

inexorably to a vote by acclamation to return Wartburg College to Waverly.

Before the day was over, St. Paul-Luther suffered a similar fate: it, too, was closed and its students encouraged "to attend the school at the new location." This verdict was especially galling in view of the fact that the chair of the St. Paul board was Oswald Hardwig of Waverly. During debate, Hardwig took the position that the school he served had no future and ought to be closed. St. Paul-Luther constituents understandably believed that they had been sold out to Waverly interests by a traitor in their midst.

Oswald Hardwig chaired the St. Paul-Luther board at the time of the 1934 convention. His support for closing St. Paul-Luther left the college feeling betrayed.

But the deed was done. Within months Wartburg College would once again be at home in Waverly. And St. Paul-Luther would be little more than a memory. The Waverly community and constituency were understandably elated; sentiment in Clinton and St. Paul quickly moved from disbelief to anger and from anger to a search for scapegoats. How could it have happened? Who was responsible?

It may be asserted by some that God has spoken in [the decision to locate the college in Waverly] through the church. We, however, are firmly convinced that God does not resort to such methods to direct His Church in so important a matter.

From a statement (1939) by four ALC clergy with close ties to St. Paul-Luther College

For those not inclined to suspect the worst, the answer was simple. The church had committed itself in 1932 to plan for a single college in the Midwest. While the Board of Christian Higher Education had backed away temporarily from this mandate, it was ready by October 1934 to move toward implementation. ALC President C. C. Hein was determined to do the same; so was virtually every convention delegate from the eastern states. Neither Clinton nor St. Paul-Luther had facilities that could accommodate a major consolidation. On the other hand, convention delegates could see for themselves that Waverly's physical plant was adequate for at least the immediate future. The decision in favor of Waverly was obvious and inevitable—and, therefore, overwhelming.

Partisans of St. Paul-Luther and Clinton found it impossible to swallow this kind of logic. Some were ready to blame "church politics" or "steam roller tactics." Others believed that Clinton was the victim of "secret chess moves" by some combination of the "friends of Waverly," the Board for Christian Higher Education, and the president of the church. More than a few Clintonians found in the Waverly convention confirmation of their suspicions that church leadership in Ohio intended to get rid of *all* ALC colleges in the Midwest. Since Clinton had the strongest prospects for the future, it needed to be eliminated first. This was accomplished by combining the two Wartburg colleges there in 1933 and then arguing against the adequacy of Clinton's physical plant. The subsequent removal to Waverly not only eliminated Clinton; it also placed the college in a small community where it would surely die. The decisions of the church at Fond du Lac and Waverly, so the argument went, were intended to rid the church of Wartburg College without having to kill it.

This display *(below)* was part of the effort to "keep Wartburg in Clinton."

[It was] the most shameful piece of ecclesiastical skullduggery I have ever encountered: the removal of the college to a mudhole named Waverly, Iowa.

Clinton alumnus Hans Groth (1966), remembering the 1934 ALC convention

courtesy: Mary Ellen Hein

Just as the decision of 1932 had left an opening for Waverly, so also the decision of 1934 offered a few rays of hope for both St. Paul and Clinton. Once again the new location was provisional only; Wartburg College was to be "continued" in Waverly, but Waverly was not designated as the permanent location. Even those who believed that the college could survive in Waverly seemed open to the prospect of moving it again—perhaps when depression days were over.

The possibility of yet another move encouraged friends of St. Paul-Luther to hope against hope that the church might come back to St. Paul in permanently locating its midwestern college. Clinton partisans, on the other hand, were determined that there should be no move at all—that the college should never leave Clinton. President Proehl, whose initial response to the events at Waverly was careful and measured, soon found himself leading, but not always controlling, a furious campaign to undo the church's decision in favor of Waverly.

Almost immediately, the Wartburg faculty requested an investigation; so did pastors of the church's Illinois District. Four Wartburg students distributed a pamphlet to hundreds of congregations,

charging ALC President C. C. Hein with biased and slanderous behavior in chairing the Waverly convention and asking for a reconsideration of the decision to move the college. (One of the four, Merritt Bomhoff, became later in life a vice-president and regent at Wartburg in Waverly!) Proehl submitted to the church a list of grievances; his brother filed charges against the president of the Iowa District. Charges led to counter-charges, to petitions and hearings and investigations. When Clinton partisans went to court to challenge the legitimacy of the new Wartburg Board of Regents, the ALC responded by securing a temporary injunction prohibiting interference with the college's move to Waverly. During the early months of 1935, the whole church was in an uproar over "the Wartburg College matter."

Proehl was a fighter, and he pulled no punches. When it was suggested that he ought to be a candidate for president of the "new" Wartburg College, he issued a statement requesting "that my name be used in no connection with the dubious project of an alleged Wartburg College at Waverly." In a letter to 1,700 ALC pastors, he warned of "the impending destruction of all schools in the middle west" as a result of the "deceptive policy of the

Everyone gathered for one last picture in Clinton, 1935.

Board of Education and secret maneuvering of church officials" who "resort to secrecy and threats against individuals." "The college at Waverly cannot succeed," he predicted. And then, with an eye to his audience, "What will happen to our seminary at Dubuque?"

The trench warfare in the church was mirrored on the Clinton campus. Students and faculty

Old Prince had
remarkable horse-
sense. You could lead
Old Prince to water,
but he refused to go
to Waverly—alive.

*Student comment on the
death of Clinton's
beloved campus horse
(spring of 1935)*

overwhelmingly supported Proehl in his effort to "save our school." Prayers offered in chapel asked God to change the hearts of those who were doing wrong to Clinton and to "deliver us from corrupt politics." Most faculty, however, were careful as to where and when they displayed their convictions. And there were some dissenters– both in the student body and in the faculty. The "Other Four," consisting of students who had attended either St. Paul-Luther or Wartburg Normal, openly challenged the "Four Students" whose widely distributed pamphlets had sought to save the college (and the church) from the curse of Waverly. John Hiltner, who had come to Clinton from Waverly in 1933, accused his faculty colleagues of disloyalty to the church and of fostering student rebellion. Hiltner paid the price; he soon found life on the Wartburg campus a "veritable hell." By the spring of 1935 he found it "impossible to go on" and left the campus— in the middle of a semester and without notifying President Proehl. Within weeks, Hiltner received a call to chair the Department of Religion at the new Wartburg in Waverly! Proehl, understandably, was furious.

The final months at Clinton were a disheartening experience for everyone concerned. Emotions on

both sides were rubbed raw. Dissenters felt threatened. Trust was in short supply. Some faculty
members were invited to accompany the college
to Waverly; others were not. And the strategy of
taking on the church got almost nowhere. An
ALC committee charged with investigating the
"Wartburg College matter" found that the 1934
convention action had been "in all respects regular,
valid, and fair," and that the charges against ALC
President C. C. Hein and others were "unwarranted."
While many in the church found these conclusions
less than persuasive, fewer and fewer seemed to
be interested in continuing the struggle. The
decision to merge the colleges in Waverly was
neither reversed nor put on hold.

By the summer of 1935, the high-stakes contest
was essentially over. The college in Clinton was
closed. Proehl tried for several years to find ways
of "organizing the forces," but he recognized that
there was "little promise of wholehearted
response." He had fought as hard as he possibly
could for his college, but "the bells were rung
down on us."

Proehl was understandably bitter, not only over
"seeing one's life-work destroyed," but also because
of the "blistering fire of provocation" which he had
been made to endure. And he had no enthusiasm
for the "surreptitious venture" in Waverly that was
intended to carry on the Wartburg tradition.
Fifteen years later, on the occasion of its centennial,
Wartburg College invited Otto Proehl to be the
recipient of an honorary degree. Proehl declined.
"Let us not invite new futilities," he said.

CHAPTER FIVE

A Sense of Place

The American Lutheran Church decided in October 1934 to close its campuses in Clinton and St. Paul the following summer, and to "continue" Wartburg College in Waverly. The word "continue" was a useful legal construct that enabled the church to move the name, the charter, and perhaps accreditation from one place to another. But the decision also made reference to the "new four-year college" in Waverly. What the architects of change had in mind was an institution that would reflect the traditions of both Clinton and St. Paul, but that would carry along only a portion of the institutional baggage from each. The "new" Wartburg would have a new board, chosen from the two existing boards, a new president, and a new faculty. It was to be a four-year college, offering "only the minimum number of majors required for accreditation."

All of this change needed to be accomplished in a matter of months. It would have been a daunting assignment in the best of times. But the early months of 1935, with their constant drumbeat of agitation over the "college question," were the worst of times. Otto Proehl, convinced that the whole undertaking was corrupt and that the new board of regents was illegitimate, refused to cooperate. Many observers doubted that college doors in Waverly would swing open in the fall of 1935. In some quarters this was a fear; in Clinton, it was still a hope.

Contributing to the mood of discouragement was the inability of the new board to find a new president. Norman Menter, a pastor from Detroit then serving on the Board of Christian Higher Education, was elected to the position in late January 1935. Unfortunately, Menter spent the next four months trying to decide what to do. Along the way, he declined the presidency, was induced to reconsider, and agreed to serve as acting president while making a final decision. In this temporary role, Menter functioned mostly *in absentia*. A Waverly board member, Oswald Hardwig, did his best to stay on top of day-to-day responsibilities.

In April, the *Clinton Herald* gleefully reported an admission by Menter that the removal of Wartburg College from Clinton was a mistake. Another report had Menter saying, "Waverly is not the place for the school permanently even if it has the buildings. You cannot build up a school in a little dump like that." Menter subsequently issued a statement denying that he had called Waverly a "dump," but he did acknowledge that "Waverly is not an ideal permanent location for our midwestern school." Even so, he was not yet ready to say yes or no to the presidency; apparently he was torn between a strong sense of responsibility and a simultaneous lack of enthusiasm for the Waverly challenge. By early June, board of regents members were getting more than a little impatient. "I am disgusted with Menter," advised board chair W. H. Behrens. "I doubt whether his heart is in Waverly." The scheduled opening of Wartburg in Waverly was little more than two months away. And still there was no president.

A few weeks later, and four months after his initial election, Menter finally declined the call to

become president of Wartburg College. "Let us hope that the next called man will accept," said Behrens. "Very much valuable time has been lost."

Indeed. But not everything was lost. During the months of presidential indecision, Menter and the board took a number of steps to prepare for the return of Wartburg to Waverly. August Engelbrecht

courtesy: Wartburg Theological Seminary

Norman Menter waited more than four months before declining the presidency of Wartburg College.

was invited back to serve as treasurer. A curricular framework—professional and pre-professional programs on a substructure of liberal arts—gained approval. Tuition and fee charges were established. Most important, however, was the task of creating a faculty. Since faculty members at both St. Paul-Luther and Clinton were to be terminated as of July 1, 1935, the pool of candidates appeared strong. Selection, however, was based not only on the usual qualifications, but also on commitment to the new enterprise in Waverly. As a result, some talented members of the Clinton faculty were eliminated from consideration. Martin Wiederaenders, Gerhard Ottersberg, and Albert Aardal were among those initially not invited,

G. J. Neumann,
dean, vice-president,
beloved teacher,
and poet

I will not vote for the appointment of any man, no matter how capable, unless and until I have assurance from him that he is heart and soul in favor of the college which the church has decreed shall be opened here [in Waverly] in September. Any member of the faculty who is coming here with a battle-axe on his shoulder or a gun in his pocket, will get no comfort from me when it comes to confirming his appointment.

Board secretary
Oswald Hardwig (1935)
on building a faculty
for Wartburg in Waverly

was incredibly strong—and almost exclusively male. From Clinton came not only Hiltner, Wiederaenders, Ottersberg, and Aardal, but also G. J. Neumann, A. W. Swensen, Elmer Hertel, and A. D. Cottermann. Alfred Haefner was called from Wartburg Seminary; Ernest Heist, who had taught at Wartburg Normal, returned to service. Four members of the St. Paul-Luther faculty (in addition to master custodian Charles Pichelmeyer, who was called a bit later) received appointments: John Chellevold, Herman Kuhlmann, Carl Muench, and Jacob Cornils. Cornils was serving at the time as acting president of St. Paul-Luther; in contrast to Otto Proehl in Clinton, he had made no effort to defy the church in the heartbreaking task of closing down his school.

The spring and summer of 1935 was a time of painful good-byes in Clinton and St. Paul; in Waverly it was a season of desperation. Not until July 17 was a president finally chosen; before the day was over, Edward Braulick had accepted the call. He had little more than a month to get the

presumably because of their pro-Clinton inclinations. Only after other candidates proved to be unavailable were the three given opportunity to continue their distinguished careers in Waverly.

Whatever the standards, the faculty that was assembled during the spring and summer of 1935

Wartburg's Faculty Gathers For Opening of New College

Shown here are twenty of the members of the faculty of Wartburg College.
Those pictured are as follows, left to right:
Back row: (1) Prof. A. A. Aardal, head of department of physics; (2) Prof. A. E. Cotterman, head of the department of Latin; (3) Rev. R. C. Schlueter, student pastor; (4) Dr. J. H. Hiltner, head of the department of religion and philosophy; (5) Prof. J. Cornils, head of the department of German; (6) Dr. Martin Wiederanders, registrar and head of the department of education; (7) the Rev. E. J. Braulick, president; (8) Dr. G. J. Neumann, dean of the college and head of the department of English; (9) Miss Katherine Kaiser, dean of women, and instructor in Latin and physical education for women; (10) Aug. Engelbrecht, treasurer.

Front Row: (1) Dr. A. E. Haefner, head of the department of Greek and librarian; (2) the Rev. A. H. Braun, field director; (3) Prof. Alvin C. Fritz, dean of men, instructor in the department of education; (4) Prof. J. O. Chellevold, professor of mathematics; (5) Prof. Elmer W. Hertel, director of athletics and instructor in biology; (6) Prof. A. W. Swenson, head of the department of chemistry; (7) Prof. Carl Muench, head of the commerce department; (8) Prof. H. J. Kuhlmann, assistant professor in the department of English; (9) Prof. Gerhard Ottersburg, head of the department of history; (10) Prof. E. G. Heist, head of the music department.
Not shown are J. Willman Thalman, voice instructor, and Miss Marlys Schwarck, instructor of violin and orchestra.

Waverly faculty
assembled for the
reopening of the
college in Waverly.

college up and running. Some of the faculty had already arrived in Waverly; in the absence of leadership, they were making decisions on their own. John Chellevold was called from St. Paul-Luther to teach physics; Albert Aardal came from Clinton to teach mathematics. When the two met, they discovered that each would prefer the assignment of the other. So on their own, and without checking with anyone, they simply exchanged responsibilities. In the long run, their decision turned out to be highly productive. But for the moment, it was symptomatic of a critical need for leadership.

To tell the truth, the job in Waverly has so many angles to it that I could not conscientiously wish it upon my enemies.

Martin Wiederaenders (1935) on his call to Wartburg in Waverly

Braulick

Edward Braulick came to the presidency of Wartburg College with a long history of dedicated service to his church and its colleges. He had been a member of the faculties at Eureka, Wartburg Normal, and Texas Lutheran and of the Board of Trustees of Wartburg Normal College. Nothing in his experience, however, could have prepared him for the thankless assignment that he took on in Waverly. Not since the days of Friedrich Lutz

Edward Braulick successfully met the challenge of reopening Wartburg in Waverly.

had a Wartburg president faced such terrifying prospects.

It was not simply the challenge of getting the doors open in September; it was also a matter of keeping them open. This meant gathering and retaining students from a constituency that, at best, had good reason to believe the college would not long survive in Waverly, and, at worst, was openly hostile to the whole enterprise. It meant getting students in sufficient numbers to retain state accreditation. It meant figuring out how to survive in the grim world of the Great Depression.

The college had received a few thousand dollars as a relocation gift from the Waverly community; beyond that, it had no outside financial resources except for an uncertain and always inadequate subsidy from the church. Few students could afford to pay for their education. And faculty and staff who had lived for years on partial salaries, the assistance of relatives, and the patience of creditors were still finding it difficult to keep bread on their tables. For the church, the college, and almost everyone, the story always seemed to be the same: "No money."

What a time to begin a new academic enterprise! But Braulick and his colleagues had no alternative except to pull things together as best they could. They worked hard, they worked together, and they succeeded. The 1935-36 academic year got under way—in Waverly, on schedule, and with an enrollment that exceeded every expectation. A total of 166 full-time students matriculated. Transfers from Clinton numbered 27; from St. Paul-Luther the total was 18. A class of 85 first-year students provided some hope for the future.

Braulick was a conciliator—on campus and off. He reminded faculty colleagues that Waverly was no place to continue the bitter infighting of

Here at Waverly, we are coming along as well as can be expected, I suppose. An idealist does not exactly feel himself at home in the company of utilitarians.

Faculty member Alfred Haefner (1936) on his first year in Waverly

Clinton days. He made the rounds of ALC district conventions, encouraging an emphasis on college rather than on place. Even the friends of Clinton and St. Paul gave him high marks for his ability to "pour oil on troubled waters."

Every effort was made to create a spirit of unity on campus. St. Paul-Luther was affirmed by adopting its "College of Our Brightest Days" as the Wartburg loyalty song. Choosing orange and black as school colors and "Knights" as a nickname similarly recognized Wartburg's roots in Clinton. The 1935-36 college yearbook not only included the usual student portraits; for seniors it also indicated previous institutions attended. Students did not forget where they were from; but they quickly came together. The homecoming banquet in October was "absolutely sold out and jammed... the spirit shown impressed everyone."

Some of the good spirit developed out of shared adversity. The great blizzard of early 1936 blocked trains coming into Waverly, and a coal shortage quickly developed. At first, classroom temperatures were reduced; students and faculty piled on as many clothes as possible to keep warm. Eventually Luther Hall, Old Main, and the gymnasium had to be closed down for lack of coal; classes met in the residence halls. In the midst of it all, students kidded each other about being "cream puffs."

In most respects, Wartburg's first year in Waverly was a good one. Braulick, however, worried more than a little about enrollment. A number of students who had been on hand in September were gone before commencement. Some failed;

We want the spirit of forbearance and charity to rule. Our aim will be: no Clinton, no Waverly, but only a Wartburg.

Edward Braulick (July 1935) upon his election as president of Wartburg College

The St. Paul-Luther loyalty song was adopted by Wartburg.

some quit for financial reasons; a few stayed only long enough to play football. Enrollment was crucial. "If [Wartburg] grows, the cause is won. If it declines, we will have trouble to keep it at Waverly," warned L. H. Schuh, chair of the ALC Board of Education. Fortunately, enrollment increased in the fall of 1936; thereafter, it held fairly steady until World War II. Even this degree of success required faculty members willing to spend long, hot summers on the road, "beating the bushes" for students.

Finances, too, presented a continuing challenge. The church decreed "no expansion" of facilities and programs, but it made little difference. Funds were unavailable in any event. On the other hand, while "pay-as-you-go" contracts survived for a few more years, faculty salaries got paid in full. Contrary to some expectations, Wartburg in Waverly seemed to be "making it." Efforts at the 1936 ALC convention to move the college out of Waverly met with little favor. After taking another look at St. Paul and Clinton, the church in 1940 decided to designate Waverly as the location for "the midwestern senior college of the American Lutheran Church."

Hopes that this "assurance of permanence" would lead to a new era of growth were dashed a year later by the outbreak of World War II. Just as the Great Depression had dictated the possibilities of the 1930s, so the "war effort" consumed the energies and resources of the early 1940s. On the

If the church would send us students who are able to pay, we could easily break even.

Edward Braulick (1935) on the financial challenges of the Great Depression

The call to the colors is on the lips of every one of us today

Many boys have left us during the past months. For each of these boys we have the warmest feelings of respect and loyalty.

The call to the colors, however, is not limited entirely to these gallant fighting men. Wartburg has exemplified this fact in many ways. Our "V" programs bring technical training for the armed forces within our walls. Our bond drives give moral and financial support to our government. Our pre-theologians are patriotically engaged in preparation to meet the spiritual needs of our country now and later. Our war information center and special programs keep us abreast of history in the making. Our active participation in civilian defense projects has made us a part of the home front.

Here at Wartburg we realize that each of us must assume his place in the war effort.

TOWARD THIS GREAT ENDEAVOR WE DEDICATE THIS DIAMOND JUBILEE FORTRESS.

Page 8

home front almost everything except patriotism was in short supply—or completely unavailable. Inconvenience occasionally punctuated by genuine pain became a way of life for most Americans.

For Wartburg College the war was more than inconvenient. From the beginning it was clear that the "manpower needs" of the nation would mean the departure of some faculty and large numbers of male students. Between 1942 and 1943, the college lost 100 students, more than a third of its student body, primarily to the armed forces. For the first time in history, Wartburg counted more women than men on campus.

This page from the 1943 *Fortress* illustrates the spirit that permeated the campus during the war effort.

The decline in student numbers was accompanied by program reductions, by leaving vacant positions unfilled, by sending faculty on leave, and by tight-fisted control of expenditures. Not surprisingly, the campus community found itself gripped by a survival mentality. As the war drew to a close, Wartburg College almost seemed to be back where it had been in 1935. To those who had long dreamed of a "Greater Wartburg," it was all very discouraging.

Once again the familiar questions were being raised. Why was the college in Waverly? Was Waverly really the best location? Would it make sense to plan for an entirely new campus in a larger city? Perhaps the 1940 "final" decision in favor of Waverly was not so final after all. As the American Lutheran Church began to think in terms of post-war expansion, it voted in 1944 to consider alternate locations for its four-year college in the Midwest.

Some Waverly partisans attempted to deflect implied criticism of their community by suggesting that the problem was not Waverly; rather it was a lack of leadership in the college. Whatever the analysis, the church's decision to reopen again the question of location was thoroughly demoralizing. Without some sense of permanence or place, how could Wartburg College possibly get ready for the opportunities of a postwar world? How could *anyone* lead?

Becker

Amidst this cloud of uncertainty, Edward Braulick decided to resign; a few months later, in early 1945, Conrad H. Becker was elected his successor. Becker was a graduate of the proseminary program (directed by his father, Johannes) at Wartburg in Waverly, and of Wartburg Seminary. While serving as a pastor in Colorado, he earned a master's degree, and in 1940 was called to become

superintendent of the Lutheran Children's Home in Waverly. During World War II, Wartburg College invited him to teach social work on a part-time basis. He was acquainted with the college, and the college with him.

Conrad H. Becker was a tireless leader who ushered in an era of unprecedented growth.

Becker accepted the call to Wartburg College "in obedience to the Church that called me and to God, who was confronting me with a great challenge." A major part of the challenge was, in fact, the church that had called him. With the end of the war in sight, and with good prospects for postwar prosperity, Wartburg College had the opportunity to become a "Greater Wartburg." But not unless it had a place it could call home. It was time for the church to make up its mind.

Becker began immediately to articulate the same argument that Otto Proehl had used a decade earlier: "You cannot move a college." A college, said Becker, is "more than student body and faculty and buildings." Relocating Wartburg would mean "a new school with a new name, a new faculty, a new curriculum, the beginning of

In the minds of [many] the name "Waverly" is still associated with perfidy. . . . the result of sinful action. . . . Thus, to many the question of location is not one of simple economic expediency but of Christian ethics.

Former Wartburg College staff member A. H. Braun (1946) on the "college problem"

Certainly a decision of the permanent location of Wartburg must be reached now or very probably no location will be needed at all for Wartburg College.

Wartburg College Dean of Students William Roselius (1945)

a new history, new loyalty, and new traditions." Becker was prepared to play a high-stakes game. If the church was unwilling to "stand by" Wartburg College, he was prepared to resign, and, he said, ranked members of the faculty would do the same.

Becker found an ally in M. G. Neale, a North Central evaluator who was invited to make a preliminary visit to the campus in 1945. Neale's report indicated that Waverly would be a suitable location for the college—if the physical plant was substantially improved and if the campus was quadrupled in size. Neale suggested that the City of Waverly assist Wartburg in securing the additional real estate; otherwise, the church would be justified in seeking a location elsewhere. Without a campus of at least 40 acres, there would be no possibility of accreditation.

In the meantime, the church's Board of Christian Higher Education was considering six other locations: Waterloo, Fort Dodge, Dubuque, and

Sheldon in Iowa; Madison and Janesville in Wisconsin. (In addition, Becker was asked to investigate possibilities of combining Wartburg with Luther College in Decorah. Luther's terms: "You can close Wartburg and come to Decorah at any time.")

The challenge to Becker and the Waverly community was clear. Either find a way to enlarge the Waverly campus or face the prospect of losing the college to another community. As it had done so often in the past, Waverly rallied to the cause. Pledges totaling $100,000 were secured for campus expansion; St. Paul's Lutheran congregation and the Waverly Chamber of Commerce agreed to guarantee the pledges. Armed with this commitment, the Neale recommendations, and the failure of any other city to offer "as much value as we would leave behind at Waverly," the American Lutheran Church decided in early 1946 "to stay in Waverly." This time the finality of the decision was not in doubt. The college was authorized to begin

> I refuse to be the administrator of a school that is not in a position to do justice to its faculty, its students, and its constituency . . . . We have reached the turning point in the history of Wartburg College. Either our Church recognizes the needs of this institution and provides adequate ways and means for its administration or we decide that the College is not vital to the development of our church, in which case the school should be closed immediately.
>
> *C. H. Becker (1945) on the church's responsibility to Wartburg College*

Students taking it easy, circa 1950

The sounds of construction seldom stopped during the Becker years.

No one who was not then a member of the Wartburg family can have an appreciation of what North Central accreditation meant for Wartburg College. To all of us it meant that we had gained a new self-respect, that there was a future for Wartburg, that we could take our place alongside other colleges of the Middle West.

C. H. Becker (1964), remembering one of the great moments of his presidency

assembling real estate for a major expansion of the campus. The church had not only chosen Waverly; it had also come to believe in Waverly.

C. H. Becker had passed the first—and greatest—test of his presidency. Wartburg's days as an institutional transient—or, as Becker put it, "a college on wheels"—were over. It had taken nearly a century, but at long last Wartburg College knew not only where it was, but where it would stay.

After location came accreditation. The State of Iowa had accredited Wartburg since Clinton days, but North Central accreditation had always seemed out of reach. In postwar America it was clearly an absolute prerequisite for survival. Accordingly, Becker made accreditation a priority, determined that it be secured by 1948. The effort to meet North Central standards was demanding— and ultimately successful. In March of 1948, Becker reported to the campus from Chicago that North Central had added Wartburg to its list of accredited institutions. Returning by train, Becker and his

wife were met in Waterloo by an enthusiastic Wartburg/Waverly delegation. When they arrived on campus, they found the Wartburg College Band ready to lead a procession to the dining hall, where celebration continued "until long after the hour of midnight."

Becker's third major challenge involved campus and facilities. The preliminary North Central visit in 1945 had indicated the woeful inadequacy of both; buildings once described as "splendid" were now considerably less than that. Even more telling was the pressure created by the rapid increase in student numbers following World War II. The arrival on campus of former GIs helped enrollment soar from 206 students in 1945 to 489 in 1946. Thereafter, the size of the student body grew steadily; at the time of Becker's retirement in 1964 it numbered almost 1,200.

Within months of his election, Becker attempted to get several construction projects under way, but the ALC Board of Trustees refused permission,

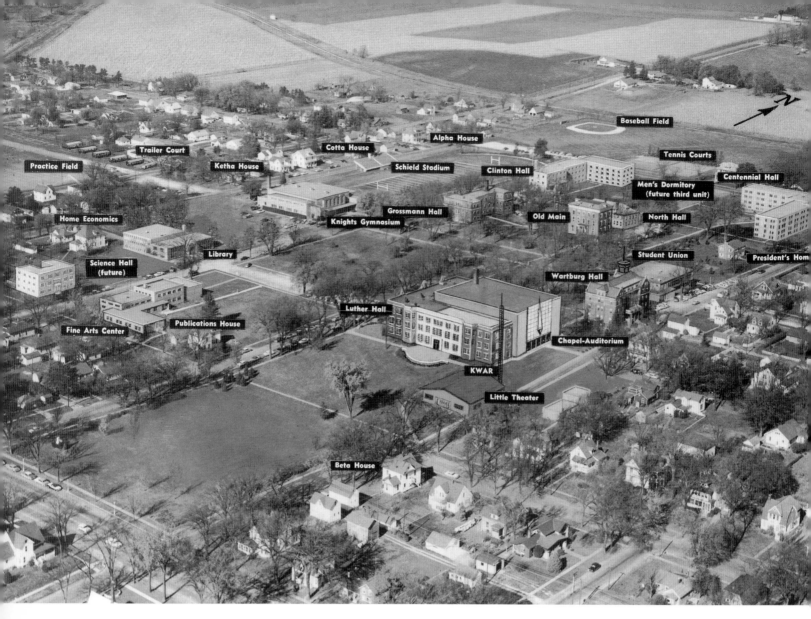

Labels on image: Baseball Field, Alpha House, Cotta House, Trailer Court, Tennis Courts, Ketha House, Schield Stadium, Clinton Hall, Centennial Hall, Practice Field, Men's Dormitory (future third unit), Home Economics, Grossmann Hall, Knights Gymnasium, Old Main, North Hall, Library, Science Hall (future), Student Union, President's Hom, Fine Arts Center, Publications House, Luther Hall, Wartburg Hall, Chapel-Auditorium, KWAR, Little Theater, Beta House

The Waverly campus quadrupled in size in the years following World War II.

pending a final decision on location of the college. When that decision came in early 1946, the church was ready both to approve and to provide assistance. Funds from the Waverly community made possible an expansion of the campus from 11 to 42 acres.

Almost every year of Becker's presidency brought with it a new or remodeled building: a fourth floor added to Wartburg Hall; a third floor to Grossmann; renovation of North Hall; Knights Gymnasium; the old gymnasium converted into the Little Theater; president's residence; maintenance building; south wing of Luther Hall; Centennial, Vollmer, and Hebron halls; Student Union and Danforth Chapel; Schield Stadium; Fine Arts; Library; Chapel-Auditorium, Clinton Hall. The sounds of construction seldom stopped. The campus was constantly in the process of becoming: new sidewalks, street closings, a trailer court for married students, conversion of residences

into student housing, the transformation of the campus from a wooded thicket into a spacious, tree-lined park.

Working night and day, and with assistance from a newly created development office, Becker personally raised much of the money for these projects. Until 1961 he could also count on construction funds from the church. The church's involvement, however, was a two-edged sword. The ALC Board of Trustees, still in the grip of a depression mentality, held to a policy of "cash on the barrelhead." Project expenditures could not exceed funds on hand at the beginning of construction; no borrowing was permitted. If bids came in higher than estimated, the project had to be correspondingly reduced in scope. Both Knights Gymnasium and the Student Union were major victims of this policy; neither could be built as originally planned.

In the late 1950s, the church changed its mind about borrowing. A new merger of Lutheran churches was in the works. By 1961 Wartburg would no longer be *the* midwestern college of the church; instead it would become one of eight. Colleges such as Luther and St. Olaf had borrowed to build up their campuses. Somehow, it seemed unfair to expect Wartburg to go into the merger with debt-free, but incomplete, facilities—and then be required indirectly to assist in paying down the indebtedness of the "Norwegian colleges." Consequently, the ALC in 1958 began authorizing Wartburg to borrow for capital projects. While helpful, the change came too late to provide any hope for merger equity.

Becker's interests extended to every facet of campus life—including the academic. His views on teaching and learning consistently reflected a deep commitment to vocation. He respected the intellect; but he was passionate about the "development of Christian character" and preparing students for lives "dedicated to the service of God and man." The role of the liberal arts was to offer "supporting programs." One of Becker's first initiatives as president was to create at Wartburg Iowa's first undergraduate program in social work. And when the college in 1951 added a component of general education to the traditional distribution requirements, a course in "Marriage and the Family" was included. More conventional developments involved new academic programs and revision of the curriculum. Along the way, Becker and his deans had remarkable success in recruiting, developing, and retaining an outstanding faculty. The student body was no less talented. Despite the emphasis on service—or more likely because of it—

Construction of the Student Union and Danforth Chapel began in 1954.

The controversial decision to permit social dancing on campus came in 1956.

As they remove the distinctions between the Church and the world, my interest in Wartburg wanes. I have discussed it with my Church Council and they are horrified at the news. I may now have to send my young people to a State School.

An Iowa pastor (1956), responding to the decision to permit social dancing on campus

Wartburg had a habit of attracting and graduating young men and women whose potential for leadership was extraordinary.

C. H. Becker was everlastingly a man on a mission. His genius lay not in his vision, but in his "infectious confidence that what needed to be done could be done." Becker's roots in the old Iowa Synod ran deep: "We want to be a good school. We want to be a Christian school. We want to be of service." He cared less about transformation than faithfulness. But his kind of dedicated, passionate faithfulness required the building of "The Greater Wartburg" to serve the educational needs of those who in turn would serve others. Bricks and mortar and curricular change were important; more essential was the building of "a community of Christian living"—or, as he often called it, "the Wartburg family."

The first fifteen years of Becker's presidency were, in the words of a veteran faculty member, "the happiest time in the history of the college." So many things had gone so well. Wartburg was "becoming something." Becker even managed to survive an onslaught of pious outrage when the college in 1956 "gave in to the students" and decided to permit social dancing on campus. As president, Becker took a terrible pounding from pastors, many of whom nevertheless continued to send their sons and daughters to Wartburg.

After 1960, things were not quite the same. The college continued to do well; but some of the old enthusiasm and energy began to fade. Becker was disappointed by the implications of the Lutheran merger: fewer dollars from the church; new college competitors. Faculty members, unhappy that

Becker Hall of Science was dedicated just four days after Becker died.

Wartburg was now regarded as a "poor relative" among Lutheran colleges in the Midwest, wanted something done about it. The Board of Regents, too, created troubles. One observer described it as "composed of people who seemed to see their roles as either doctrinal or financial watchdogs." The Alumni Board pressed Becker on a number of issues, including the need for racial diversity in the student body and faculty. And the promises of comprehensive long-range planning (the first in the college's history), as orchestrated by the Fund Fulfillment Corporation, were never quite fulfilled.

Becker kept pressing forward; there was so much still to be done. By 1964 he could no longer do it. Two decades of a "limitless outpouring of energies" and a constant disregard for his own welfare had taken their toll. In failing health, he submitted his resignation. Death came three years later, only four days before the dedication of the science building that was to bear his name.

CHAPTER SIX

Still on the Move

C. H. Becker was the last son of the Iowa Synod to serve as president of Wartburg College. But he was the first to leave to his successor a college with a reputation extending beyond the confines of church and community. During the Becker years, Wartburg entered the mainstream of American higher education. And it did so without compromising the historic commitment of "preparing young men and women for Christian living and for full-time service in the Church as well as in the various professions and vocations."

John W. Bachman succeeded C.H. Becker as president of Wartburg College in 1964.

Becker's successor, John W. Bachman, came to Wartburg College in 1964 from Union Theological Seminary in New York—a move he described as "a decision to desert the east bank of the Hudson for the west bank of the Cedar River." Bachman's roots were in the Ohio Synod; a distinguished teaching career had taken him from Capital University in Ohio to Baylor University in Texas and then to Union, where he served as Professor of Practical Theology and Director of the Center for Communication and the Arts.

As president, Bachman reaffirmed many themes of the Wartburg tradition: faith and learning, life in community, and even the Wartburg "GQ" (guts quotient) which, he said, "predict[s] the ability to stick to a task when the going gets rough." He insisted that "Wartburg make no apologies for including in our curriculum some provision for professional and pre-professional preparation. . . . The sharp separation which often appears to exist between 'making a living' and 'learning to live' reminds us that we have not yet realized Luther's sense of vocation through occupation."

But there were also unmistakable changes in nuance and direction: "Students should not be attracted to Wartburg College merely out of loyalty or sentiment; we want them to come in the conviction that they can experience here the highest possible quality of education." Academic standards ought to be higher; the distinctive relationship of faith to scholarship should be reflected in the academic enterprise. Wartburg's location and size were "conducive to conversation and contemplation," and could facilitate a "lively interdisciplinary exchange within Christian community." At the same time, it was essential that Wartburg be "opened to the world beyond Waverly"; the college ought to resist becoming "a pious haven for culturally retarded adolescents."

Bachman's enthusiasm for the life of the mind proved to be contagious. Before long student publications were quoting Kierkegaard and Bultmann; Wartburg Players began presenting plays by Albee and Ionesco; the honors program was reshaped to include student-faculty colloquia. Weekend

The Wartburg College Artist Series has provided the campus with a steady stream of memorable performances.

Wartburg has always been a college on the move; we no longer move from place to place, but, we hope, from level to level of excellence.

John Bachman (1965) on the future of Wartburg College

cultural excursions took students to galleries, concerts, and plays in Minneapolis and Chicago. Cooperative programs, as well as student and faculty exchanges, were established with other colleges and universities; a steady stream of speakers and performers—many of them international—brought to the campus, in Bachman's words, "exposure to the life and thought of the world." At his suggestion, interdisciplinary faculty "groups" replaced the traditional faculty divisional structure. Since faculty quality is "the single most important factor in the quality of a college," Bachman gave high priority to improving faculty salaries. And in 1968 the decades-old dream of a faculty sabbatical leave program finally became a reality.

The most substantial—and durable—academic innovation of the Bachman years was the implementation in 1967 of the 4-4-1 calendar (Fall, Winter, and May terms) and an entirely new curriculum to go with it. The initiative was Bachman's; he wanted to extend the range of curricular offerings and encourage off-campus experiences for students and faculty. He preferred the 4-4-1 to the then-fashionable 4-1-4 (Fall, January, and Spring terms) because of the potential for extending the May Term experience into the summer. Once in place, the new framework set off an incredible burst of faculty creativity—especially in the creation of new courses, both on and off campus, for the May Term. Whole programs, such as foreign languages, came to be built around the distinctive possibilities of the 4-4-1 calendar. A "capstone" course in "Problems of War and Peace" was introduced as a requirement for graduation.

The new calendar and curriculum did not exhaust the possibilities for innovation. Under the leadership of Ronald Alexander, a faculty-student committee proposed creation of a "satellite college" to make available to Wartburg students an alternate educational experience. Administrative support was strong; by 1972 the new program—dubbed "Chrysalis"—was in place. It offered selected first- and second-year students residence-centered learning, cross-disciplinary studies in the humanities and social sciences, and an opportunity and responsibility for shaping their own education. Students and program were housed in Wartburg Hall; course work took the form of seminars and independent study. Under the leadership of directors K. D. Briner and Herman Diers, Chrysalis

created "a different style of education"—separate but not isolated from the rest of the college community.

For many students, Chrysalis worked well. Those who completed the program tended to be enthusiastic about the experience. More than a few, however, dropped out along the way—often finding the heavy dose of student responsibility more than they were ready to assume.

Chrysalis was never without its critics; but even detractors were willing to give it credit for enhancing the quality of intellectual discourse on campus. By the late 1970s, however, general enthusiasm for the program began to wane. Fewer students seemed willing to make the necessary commitment; the college budget was tight; faculty members were preoccupied with the development of a new program in general education. No one was arguing that Chrysalis had failed; more than a few, however, were ready to suggest that perhaps it had run its

Dan Thomas led Chrysalis discussions in Wartburg Hall.

course. As the best of the Chrysalis experience came to be incorporated into a new "Wartburg Plan" of general education—thereby making it available to all Wartburg students—the case for continuing Chrysalis as a distinct program no longer seemed compelling. The decision to discontinue it came in 1980—during the final months of William Jellema's presidency. A year later Chrysalis was gone. No one rejoiced in its death; the faculty pledged to find ways of keeping alive its spirit.

John Bachman's passion for ideas and reasoned discourse was severely tested by the general disruption of American life and society during the years of his presidency. The events of the 1960s—especially the war in Vietnam and the struggle for civil rights—spawned a youth culture determined to correct the ills of American society—and to do it now. On college campuses everywhere, faculty members were drawn into prophetic roles; students found themselves moving from initial skepticism to outright rejection of inherited traditions and values. Many were convinced that it was necessary not only to "stop the war" in Vietnam, but also to "change the system"—on campus as well as in Washington, D. C. Protest became a mechanism of choice for change.

This new world of student (and faculty) activism

Herman Diers was a tireless innovator and gifted teacher.

I cannot help but admire the activist and radical, but they have not surfaced yet at this campus.

Wartburg Trumpet News Editor John Walter (November 1968)

The Vietnam era stimulated a culture of conversation – and confrontation.

The civil rights movement spurred an agenda for change.

How can you take part in a Homecoming when there's killing in Vietnam?

An unnamed student (1969) quoted in the Wartburg Trumpet

took root slowly on the Wartburg campus. During the first few years of Bachman's presidency, the college community dealt with the great issues of the day in traditional academic fashion: discussion and debate, editorials and letters to the editor, distribution of printed materials, silent vigils. Despite frequent complaints about student apathy, the campus was substantially engaged; but almost always that engagement found expression in tones of civility and respect. When in 1967 a Wartburg-Community Committee to End the War in Vietnam was formed, it made clear that it had no interest in the tactics of protest.

In 1969, the fabric of community on the Wartburg campus began to fray. African-American students cheered for the opposition at a basketball game. Shortly thereafter, a burning cross appeared on campus; anonymous phone calls told African-American students that it was intended for them. One of the candidates for student body president ran (and lost) that year on a platform of "student

power." In the fall came a passionate though unsuccessful attempt to cancel classes for a Vietnam Moratorium Day. Large numbers of students and faculty participated instead in an on-campus teach-in and a march to the county courthouse for a memorial service. The day ended with the planting of a "tree of life" on the campus.

Early in 1970, "Concerned Students for Change" presented a list of "recommendations" for broad expansion of student rights. They asked for an immediate response from the college so that students could "make plans for next year accordingly." A few months later came the tragic deaths of American students at Kent State and Jackson State. Student fury led many colleges and universities to close down before the end of the academic year. Wartburg students settled for dyeing the fountain red ("the blood of Kent") and for a week of mourning during which the American flag was lowered to half-mast (thereby infuriating local veterans organizations). Commencement was

To see one hundred or more people out yelling is beautiful— but for Outfly? This is ridiculous. Do you people realize that there is a world outside Wartburg?

Wartburg student Beth Kasten (1970), in a letter to the Wartburg Trumpet

held as scheduled; some faculty and students used it as an occasion to publicly protest the awarding of an honorary degree to the publisher of the *Waterloo Courier*.

Student discontent with the world—and with the "power structures" of the college—intensified during the early 1970s. The great issues of the day—poverty, race, student power, the draft, the war—were played out in the nation and on the campus. In the minds of some, Wartburg College was not only a candidate for change, but also a launching pad for reform of the larger society. For a few it was a convenient laboratory for confrontation.

Strategies and tactics varied from issue to issue, and from month to month. Marches on the local draft board office and sit-ins reflected a commitment to peaceful persuasion. Efforts to physically hold hostage the board of regents—or, on another occasion, the president—as a way of securing capitulation to demands did not. At one point the college quietly developed plans "to evacuate in case of threatened sabotage." And in the spring of

1972, the *Wartburg Trumpet* published a letter from a faculty member suggesting that "sometimes it takes violence on the part of protesters to expose the violence done by the authorities in Vietnam, Waterloo, Waverly, and Chicago."

Despite what sometimes seemed to be a "crisis of the month," Wartburg came through the traumatic days of the early seventies quite well. Much of the credit belongs to John Bachman. It was Bachman who set the tone for responding to campus unrest; most members of the faculty and board—and many students—pitched in.

Believing that Wartburg's commitment to the faith should make it possible to "transcend disagreement in acceptance of one another and in growth together," Bachman welcomed unrest to the campus "if its purpose was to improve rather than destroy." And in calling for "reasonable deliberations within a community of the concerned," he reminded the campus that "ultimate victories . . . are not won over persons but over ignorance and evils. If we cannot see beyond victory over blacks or

Storm clouds are again threatening us. I have been asked whether it seems to me that our school is heading into the gravest menace it has ever confronted. I cannot deny that a crisis is again looming, caused . . . by the trends of the times. I see the danger, but I am not disheartened by it. . . . Wartburg possesses an inherent toughness . . . that has carried it through perils in the past, and I have confidence that it again [will] do so in the future.

Wartburg historian Gerhard Ottersberg (1971) on the challenges of the seventies

Robert Dell was a passionate advocate for peace and justice.

whites, doves or hawks, hippies or Establishment, we will only share in defeat."

Bachman's determination that the college experience "thaw some minds . . . within a community of the concerned" was matched by a commitment to institutional change. The corollary was a resolve that "changes . . . are not hastened by attempted coercion." Early in his presidency he began taking steps to increase substantially the presence of African-Americans in the life of the college: students, faculty, staff, board, curriculum. It was not easy. Efforts to designate scholarships for minority students created a backlash among white students. Even as their numbers grew, African-American students invariably found Wartburg less than hospitable; they grew weary of being "used" to educate others. And often they regarded efforts on their behalf as superficial at best. Nevertheless, Bachman persisted. So did many members of the faculty and staff. Some minds were opened; some good things happened. In 1971, when an African-American woman, Ruth Owens, was elected Homecoming queen, everyone understood that Wartburg was changing—certainly not enough, but changing. When Bachman left the college in 1974, he and his wife, Elsie, were invited to become honorary members of the Wartburg Afro-American Society.

Bachman was also more than a little responsive to one of the consistent themes of student activists: that the college encourage and permit students to take more responsibility for their own lives. Student membership on college committees was expanded; student leaders were invited to meetings of the faculty and board of regents. Individual housing units were given authority to establish hours. Men and women began living together in the same buildings—on different floors—and were permitted to visit in each other's rooms. When the State of

There is room on this campus for both the person who believes fervently that President Nixon's military policies provide the best hope for world peace and should be supported enthusiastically, and the person who is absolutely convinced that the President has made a ghastly mistake which can only compound disaster and which should be overruled immediately.

John Bachman (1970) in a sermon marking the beginning of a "Week of Mourning"

Ruth Owens was crowned 1971 Homecoming queen.

Iowa lowered the drinking age to eighteen, the college agreed, subject to certain limitations, to permit alcohol in the residence halls. Hard drugs and marijuana were another matter; Wartburg (and local law enforcement officials) steadfastly refused to countenance their presence on campus. The college, however, did encourage and support efforts to make drug counseling available.

None of this happened without controversy. None of it came without problems. But where it counted most, it worked. Wartburg College came through the Vietnam years with its institutional integrity intact, its sense of community enhanced. It was, of course, a different kind of community: no longer "entire of itself," but continually involved in the world. For most, the experience was life-changing. Members of the Wartburg community never stopped talking with each other; only rarely did they stop listening. Despite anger and outrage, there were no injuries, no facilities destroyed. Bitter antagonists often remained friends. Bachman's faith in "continuing deliberations among people

Yes, have your free speech, but damn it, don't burn down any of our buildings.

Summary by Trumpet editor Ken Weitz (1970) of John Bachman's response to activism

who know each other well" was regularly tested; it was never forsaken.

Not everyone, of course, saw it this way. A few members of the Wartburg community continued to regard Bachman and his administrative team as reactionary "tools of the Establishment." On the other hand, more than a few—both on and off campus—were disappointed by his unwillingness to crack down on student dissent and professorial arrogance, and by changes in student life which they regarded as an "experiment in permissiveness." In addition, it was deceptively easy to connect the college's policy decisions with a decline in enrollment from a record 1,450 students in 1968 to a disappointing 1,290 in 1973.

Nevertheless, even critics were willing to give Bachman his due. When he resigned in 1974 to accept a call to serve in the national office of the American Lutheran Church, most recognized that Wartburg had indeed moved "from level to level of excellence." Faculty and board had been strengthened. Creative academic programs brought national recognition. The campus had been expanded, and a half-dozen buildings or major additions had been completed. (Along the way, North Hall mercifully fell victim to the wrecking ball!). Bachman and board chair Harry Hagemann opened doors to resources in nearby Waterloo by enlisting leaders of that community into the service of the college. Though few recognized it at the time, Bachman was an architect of the Iowa Tuition Grant program—which over the years has delivered $40 million in financial assistance to Wartburg students. For all these achievements, however, nothing was more important to the life and future of Wartburg College than the leadership he demonstrated on the long, difficult walk through that valley of American life called Vietnam.

By the end of Bachman's presidency in 1974, Wartburg had come to know the world. The world, however, did not know Wartburg—at least not very well. Despite efforts by both Becker and Bachman to enlarge the constituency of the college, the connections that counted were still mostly identified with church, and alumni, and locality.

Jellema

In electing William W. Jellema the fourteenth president of Wartburg College, the board of regents signaled an intention to move the college in new directions. Theologically educated in the Reformed tradition, and with a Ph.D. in philosophy from the University of Edinburgh, Jellema brought to the college a national reputation built upon research and writing in the field of private higher education. He had experience, he had expertise, and he had connections. He was not, of course, "in the tradition," but many were inclined to believe

William W. Jellema brought to Wartburg College a national reputation in higher education.

that he could lead the college from old answers to new questions. And the realization that Wartburg could attract a man of his stature provided an invitation to great expectations.

Jellema was eager for the challenge. Wartburg seemed to him to be the kind of institution that would respond to his leadership. It was "a very good college, not fully aware itself of how good it was, let alone what its potential was."

Unfortunately, it was "still thinking about its past, thinking of itself as though [it] were 'Kraut Hill.'" He was dismayed by what he took to be a pervasive willingness to accept less than the best; the prevailing spirit was contentment with the notion that "it's good enough for Wartburg." The college was mired in mediocrity; it "seemed almost blithely unaware of how precarious its position was." Financially, it was "playing penny ante in a high stakes game." And the historic base and ownership of the college was "too narrow to sustain it in the future." Wartburg still had a lot of growing to do; growing up required "greater freedom to grow out." The challenge of presidential leadership was "to help Wartburg come through its teenage years as swiftly and with as much grace as possible," to "share the college with a broader constituency," and to "make of this college a nationally prominent institution." This meant moving quickly. With enrollment down and only "pitiful financial reserves," Wartburg "didn't have all the time in the world." It had reached a "point of no return."

Jellema was determined to transform Wartburg College; his prescriptions for change, however, were scarcely radical. He wanted, and got, a new administrative team—in some cases several times over. Believing that Wartburg had a reputation as a "party school," he sought to improve the quality of student life. His dean of students, Kent Hawley, led a successful effort to increase dramatically the numbers of international students. Early in his presidency, Jellema attempted to sharpen the identity of the college and to capitalize on its German and Lutheran roots by identifying it as "The Wartburg." (Many students and alumni saw it otherwise; they took his initiative to be an unwelcome scheme to "rename" their college by presidential fiat.)

I was looking for a college that would be a substantial challenge—but which strong presidential leadership might save and strengthen.

William Jellema (2001) on his decision to accept the presidency of Wartburg College

Wartburg's
international
student population
increased
dramatically under
the leadership
of Kent Hawley
(top right).

THE Jellema

*Student banner hung
on the president's
residence in response
to "The Wartburg"*

"The Wartburg" was introduced in tandem with "Berufung," a program designed to provide an integrated approach to student development around the theologically rooted idea of "vocation." Conceptually brilliant, "Berufung" nevertheless suffered much the same fate as "The Wartburg." It was identified as the president's program; faculty and staff never developed much sense of ownership. Students had difficulty in understanding what was in it for them. And it was easy to poke fun at a word out of the German/Lutheran tradition which most could neither understand nor pronounce.

Much of William Jellema's energy came to be focused on efforts to prepare the college for the fiscal and physical challenges of the future. Early in his presidency, he led a major effort to beautify the campus and to plan for its long-term development. Recognizing the immediate and critical need for indoor physical education facilities, he pushed relentlessly toward completion of the largest building project the college had ever seen—the Physical Education Center (dubbed the "Bionic Barn" by the *Wartburg Trumpet*). Financing arrangements for the center were unusually creative; they won for the college a national award and widespread recognition.

Construction of the P.E. Center was facilitated also by the remarkable success of "The Design for Tomorrow," at the time the most ambitious and successful fund-raising effort in the history of the college. In the process, Jellema was able to enlist support from important new constituencies—particularly in the business and foundation communities.

"Design for Tomorrow" generated substantial new revenues for the college; most were necessarily committed to specific physical and academic projects. Other potential sources of new money turned out to be less productive. The college's miniscule endowment grew only a little (though some important commitments for the future were put into place). And while student enrollment initially was stabilized, it slipped further near the end of Jellema's presidency.

Efforts to generate new funds were, however, joined to reallocation of existing resources. Jellema was determined from the outset to implement a program of "dynamic productivity and instructional cost reduction." The time had come to "phase out programs which are no longer central to the mission of the college in order to reallocate scarce resources to those which are." The days of "dynamics by accretion" were over. "The future will require dynamics by substitution—or even subtraction."

Although the promise of "dynamic productivity" was never fully realized (in part, perhaps, because the college was served by five academic deans

in six years), it did provide a context for some predictably controversial reductions in program and in faculty/staff positions—including termination of a tenured faculty member. Chrysalis was phased out; on the other hand, several new programs, including music therapy and cooperative education (combining study and work experience), were introduced. And in 1980 the faculty adopted the "Wartburg Plan," a distinctive and distinguished program in general education that provided common curricular experiences for Wartburg students for two decades to come.

The Jellema years were productive years; but they were not happy years—on campus at least. Jellema believed that an academic community ought to be "a yeasty place; a feisty place." In a sense, he got his wish. Unfortunately, however, the campus turned out to be less an exciting market-place of ideas than a fractured community in pain. Almost from the outset, faculty found it easy to believe that the new president had little respect

We are distressed about an increasing trend that seems to be excluding the faculty from the process of decision-making on our campus.

Faculty resolution (1976)

Physical Education Center (1978)

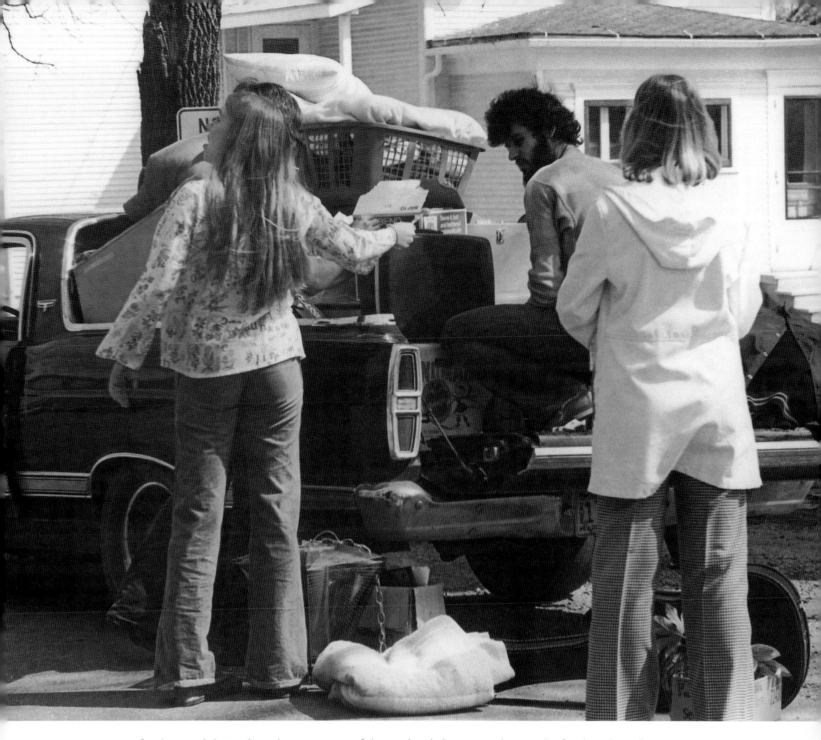

for them and their role in the governance of the college. He seemed determined not only to have his own way, but also to avoid consultation along the way. Relationships between faculty and president quickly deteriorated; efforts to repair them regularly failed.

For a time, the focus of faculty discontent was the matter of merit pay. Mandated by the board of regents during Jellema's first year, responsibility for its implementation (salary increases "to the most deserving") was bravely assumed by the president. Faculty opposition was instant and almost unanimous. Over the next several years,

battle lines were drawn. The faculty adopted resolution after resolution in opposition to merit pay. It requested outside mediation; the request was rejected by president and board. Some members of the faculty began to talk of organizing a union; many favored (but never quite consummated) a formal vote of no confidence; a few chose to leave in order to seek more attractive career opportunities elsewhere.

So long as the contest was framed in terms of struggle between president and faculty, it was easy enough for non-participants to give the president the benefit of the doubt—to understand faculty opposition as an effort to put academic privilege before institutional progress. In the eyes of one board member, faculty were "spoiled brats."

But as the trail of disillusionment grew longer and as the erosion of trust began to seep into other constituencies—students, staff, alumni, the Waverly community—the board of regents took notice. So did William Jellema. In late 1979, he announced that he would not accept another term as president of Wartburg College and would return instead to a career in scholarly research, writing, and consulting. Word of the decision was headlined in a December issue of the *Wartburg Trumpet* that included on the same page a Christmas greeting: carolers singing "Joy to the World." More than a

few readers were ready to believe (mistakenly, as it turned out) that the greeting had been designed to serve quite another purpose.

It was no credit to the Wartburg community that so many were so ready to celebrate the departure of a president who had done so many things so very well. In non-Wartburg circles, William Jellema was widely recognized as an eloquent and dynamic leader who had moved the college to new levels of distinction. But on campus (and among many alumni) he had become the persistent adversary who was neither trusting nor trusted. Despite an evident interest in the words of the Wartburg tradition, he never seemed to understand the music. And that made all the difference.

Raymond Harms taught religion and Greek from 1958 until his retirement in 1994.

Vogel

It also made possible the election in 1980 of Robert
Vogel as the fifteenth president of Wartburg College.
Vogel was not an academic; he had no experience
in higher education administration; he possessed
almost none of the standard credentials for leadership of a college. On the other hand, his career as
pastor and church executive testified to uncommon
leadership abilities. He was an alumnus; Wartburg
seemed eager for "one of our own." What especially
commended his candidacy was his sense about the
place and his enthusiasm for the possibilities of
giving new life to the Wartburg tradition.

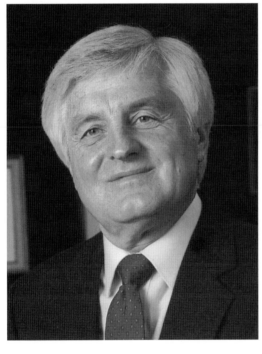

Robert Vogel,
great-grandson of
Otto Kraushaar,
accepted the
presidency in 1980.

Vogel's inauguration was an exhilarating exercise
in rebuilding community. To each college constituency he promised, "I will listen and learn from
you." He reaffirmed the "'Wartburg Spirit,' the
spirit of devotion, learning, and service to others."
Remembering the "dedication, sacrifice, stubborn
tenacity, and service" of those who had gone before,
he pledged that Wartburg would "boldly claim
the future."

During the eighteen years of his presidency
(1980-1998), Vogel regularly drew upon the
Wartburg saga for inspiration and understanding:
"We stand on the shoulders of those who came
before." His annual reports carry titles such as
"The Wartburg Spirit," "The Wartburg Story,"
"The Valiant Struggle to Emerge," "Faithful to our
Calling." Remembering, however, did not mean
reliving; Vogel was careful never to mistake the
past for the future. "Reclaiming the tradition"
involved "taking old impulses and finding new
expressions of them." He looked steadfastly forward,
and he did it with an excitement that was
contagious. Wartburg, he said, could realize and
exceed its "grandest dreams."

Whatever their source, those dreams invariably
came to be shaped by the quality of Vogel's imagination. He knew how to create an image of what
Wartburg might become, to make that image
exciting and compelling, and to enlist others in
the effort to give it life. This meant transforming
vision into shared vision; it also required a willingness to make tough decisions.

Some priorities were immediate and inescapable.
The college was, to be sure, artfully living within its
means, but an endowment of less than $2 million
was scarcely a base from which to do very much
dreaming. Even more critical was enrollment.
After reaching a peak of 1,450 students in 1968,
it had slowly declined to 1,108 in 1980. Unless
student numbers could be turned around, nothing
else would matter very much.

Admissions and retention became Vogel priorities—not only at the outset but throughout his
presidency. After a momentary decline to 1,080
students in 1981, enrollment moved steadily
upward, reaching 1,541 (almost entirely full-time)
by the time of Vogel's retirement in 1998.
Annual increases in the size of the student body

For all that has
been . . . . Thanks!
For all that will be
. . . . Yes, Yes, YES!

*From the inaugural
response of Robert Vogel
(1980)*

Greenwood, acquired in 1986, was restored to serve as the president's residence. Robert and Sally Vogel were its first occupants.

did wonders for campus and alumni morale; ever larger pools of tuition dollars—together with careful attention to how they were spent—encouraged an unprecedented sense of institutional well-being.

Scarcely less significant were successes in fundraising. Vogel embraced and continued "The Design for Tomorrow" campaign begun by his predecessor. By the time of its conclusion in 1986, the program had raised $21 million for capital projects, current operations, and endowment.

Several years of institutional planning followed, providing the basis for a new "mission driven, project focused" approach called "The Decade of Opportunity." It, too, was highly successful, not only in providing funding for capital projects, but in stimulating the creation of a number of endowed

faculty chairs and professorships. By the end of Vogel's presidency, the overall size of the endowment had grown from less than $2 million to more than $25 million.

Despite Herculean efforts by Becker, Bachman, and Jellema, Wartburg College in the early 1980s was still in a deficit position when it came to facilities. Old buildings were in need of renovation and expansion. Wartburg Hall was no longer habitable. The condition of Old Main was embarrassing. Additional classrooms and residence halls were essential to meet the needs of a growing student body. Like his predecessors, Vogel had no choice but to become a builder. Not that he was reluctant. He recognized the importance of facilities in providing quality experiences for students. And he

The Wartburg Chapel, *(right)* was a crowning achievement of Robert Vogel's presidency.

was convinced that a constant stream of construction projects, both large and small, helped build a sense of "movement and momentum."

And so Wartburg built, year after year, project after project. Vogel knew not only how to dream, but how to transform dreams into plans, and plans into reality—including a firm insistence on fiscal discipline at every step of the way.

First came the Whitehouse Business Center, Bookstore, and Visitors Center—and with them the beginnings of the campus skyway system. The long-awaited renovation of Old Main was quickly followed by an addition to the P.E. Center. A decision to use the president's residence as the center for a new student residence complex led to the acquisition, just north of the campus, of the Greenwood estate to serve as home for presidents and their families. The third floor of Luther Hall was completely renovated to create a Humanities Center. In the early 1990s came the Fine Arts Center and the McElroy Communication Arts Center, followed by the Wartburg Chapel, a new Grossmann Hall (together with the renovation and renaming of old Grossmann as Founders Hall),

and the Rada-Aleff Classroom Technology Center. Streets were closed; the entire south campus was reconfigured; and the skyway system was extended through most of the major academic buildings. The final and largest project was a new library. Ground-breaking came on the occasion of Vogel's retirement; a year later the magnificent new facility was dedicated as the Robert and Sally Vogel Library.

Alongside these major projects came a host of smaller ones—remodeling, real estate acquisitions, landscaping, sidewalks, parking, athletic facilities. Less obvious were miles of new cabling installed to connect an increasingly technology-oriented campus.

For all of his apparent love of planning and building, Vogel's great passion was for students. As president he judged almost everything in terms of its potential to contribute to the student experience at Wartburg; he kept reminding colleagues to do the same. On one level this meant articulating a clear statement of mission that could be etched into the very soul of the community: "Wartburg College is dedicated to challenging and nurturing students for lives of leadership and service as a

Grossmann Hall, dedicated in 1995, carried the name of the college's founder to a new structure.

William Waltmann, who taught mathematics at Wartburg for 43 years, helped students "put it all together."

spirited expression of their faith and learning." It involved a decision by the board of regents to stake Wartburg's future on continuing to be "an undergraduate, liberal arts, residential college of the church." It meant articulating again and again the distinctive character of a Wartburg education. Vogel talked often of the way in which the Wartburg experience enables students to make connections in their lives: "to put it all together"; to "discover and claim their callings." Wartburg, he said, is "a place that helps spark a fire, a passion, in the hearts of students and challenges them to lead and to serve."

Vogel's commitment to students was more than a matter of words. He identified with their interests and aspirations: by increasing the size of student services staff; by adding a leadership emphasis to the college's historic commitment to service; by enthusiastic presence at student events; by championing a major expansion of off-campus and internship experiences (including creation of

Wartburg West, an innovative urban program in Denver, Colorado); and even by defending the beloved tradition of Outfly against periodic faculty onslaughts!

Determined that Wartburg become a more diverse community, Vogel created a Minority Advisory Council (MAC) to provide not only counsel and assistance—but some prodding as well. He and his colleagues worked hard at connecting with the minority community in nearby Waterloo. Out of these and other efforts came not only a dramatic increase in minority student numbers, but also the Waterloo Teachers Project, an award-winning program offering adults in that community the opportunity to become teachers. A brainchild of faculty member Les Huth and board member Walter Cunningham, the program turned out to be a phenomenal success. Nearly all participants persisted to graduation; most became teachers in area schools.

Six dynamic interactions mark the distinctive character of a Wartburg education:

• A dedication to the liberal arts and a concern for usefulness and careers.

• A rigorous academic program and an emphasis on "living your learning."

• A focus on the future and an appreciation for history and heritage.

• A commitment to leadership and a tradition of service to others.

• A spirit of inquiry and exploration and a foundation of faith and values.

• A vigorous global outreach and strong Midwestern roots.

From the Wartburg Vision Statement (1987, 1991)

Another of Vogel's passions was international education—students from abroad coming to campus and Wartburg students going overseas. Both kinds of experience had deep roots in the traditions of the Iowa Synod. Each had been resurrected by C. H. Becker and expanded during the Bachman and Jellema years. By the early 1980s the number of students coming from abroad was steadily growing; Vogel kept the momentum going when he moved Dean of Students Kent Hawley into a full-time responsibility for recruiting international students. Students from abroad soon numbered more than 100, representing more than thirty countries.

One of Vogel's dreams was to get every Wartburg student overseas at least once prior to graduation. Realization of the dream never proved feasible; but the effort nevertheless provided dramatic results. May Term courses offering overseas experiences multiplied rapidly—as did study-abroad and internship programs around the globe. Tours by

music organizations took increasing numbers of students to Europe. Particularly significant was the leadership of faculty member Herman Diers in developing an experientially based program designed to provide service-learning opportunities for Wartburg students—and faculty—in developing communities. Initially focused on Tanzania, the program has since been expanded to other countries—and to multicultural settings within the United States as well.

Thanks to this kind of vision, global studies at Wartburg came to have a special and distinctive character. They were another example of "reclaiming the tradition" by finding new expressions for old—indeed old Iowa Synod—impulses of service and learning, and doing so by connecting to the world beyond Waverly.

There was, of course, much more during the Vogel years: solid finances; new academic programs; repeated national recognition of Wartburg as a

A May Term archaeological dig at Bethsaida became one of Wartburg's most popular courses abroad.

college of distinction; internationalization of the board of regents; productive reconnects with Neuendettelsau, Eisenach, and the Wartburg Castle. And always, and in every way, a commitment to the integrity of the "whole student experience."

Robert Vogel believed in "putting it all together." That was not only his expectation for students; it also lay at the heart of his leadership. Never before had there been such clarity of vision. Never before in the history of the college had so many things gone so well. Never before had Wartburg

College looked so good to so many. Vogel was ever generous in giving credit to others: faculty, staff, board, students, alumni, friends—as well as to "those who had come before." For eighteen years, however, it was he who put it all together and made it work. He never stopped trying to find new ways of breathing new life into the tradition. By the time of his retirement in 1998, Wartburg College—for the first time in its history—had become a bold and confident place, more than ready to take on the challenges of a new millennium.

Tanzania was the first destination for Venture Education, a service-learning concept developed by Herman Diers.

Ohle

To lead the college into the new century, the board of regents turned to Jack R. Ohle, senior vice president for external affairs at Drake University. Following seminary and graduate studies, Ohle had spent much of his career directing institutional advancement at colleges and universities in Ohio, Nebraska, and Iowa. His record as a fund-raiser was an invitation to high expectations; so also was his deep commitment to faith and learning.

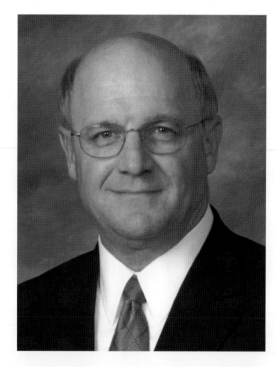

Jack R. Ohle sought to achieve "new levels of excellence" at Wartburg.

From the very outset, Ohle indicated his enthusiasm for the "great reputation and tradition" of Wartburg College. What was required was not some change in direction, but rather moving the college to "new levels of excellence." As Ohle saw it, Wartburg's historic determination to live within its means meant that "not everything that needed to be done had been done." "Wartburg," he said, "can be anything it wants to be." At the moment, however, it "did not measure up to the almost certain demands of the future." In his

inaugural address, he quoted Martin Luther: "We are not yet what we should be but we are growing toward it."

Ohle made it clear from the beginning that he did not arrive in Waverly with all of the answers. During his first year as president, he encouraged the board of regents to launch a major long-range planning initiative called Commission Wartburg. Designed to create a "framework for the future," it came to involve several hundred members of the campus community and various college constituencies. Eight task forces, each meeting several times over the course of a year, developed 266 recommendations; the board of regents subsequently assigned a priority to each. The result was a comprehensive agenda for the future, together with some clues as to how expensive that future might become.

Commission priorities became the cornerstone of Campaign Wartburg, an $88 million fundraising campaign announced at the beginning of the college's sesquicentennial year for the purpose of "celebrating a proud tradition; creating a purposeful future." Goals of the campaign included growth of the endowment to $100 million by the year 2010. This, together with an expanded annual fund, would provide financial resources for many of the programmatic priorities identified by Commission Wartburg. In addition, major facility projects were identified as part of the campaign: a new outdoor athletic complex, a renovated and enlarged science facility, a greatly expanded Student Union, a new maintenance building, and a new south entrance to the campus. Taken together, these capital projects dwarfed anything the college had ever seen or even contemplated. Encouraged by the early response to Campaign Wartburg, the college arranged a $50

The Robert and Sally Vogel Library, *(right)* constructed during Ohle's presidency, is one of the major projects that reshaped the campus.

President Jack R. Ohle
and his wife, Kris,
extended regular
invitations to
students for informal
gatherings in
their home.

Through
Wartburg's kinetic
history, through
locations and
realities of the past
150 years, our
college's leaders,
faculty, and students
kept their hearts,
minds, and energy
focused on the
purpose of our
college: "To
challenge and
nurture students
for lives of leader-
ship and service as
a spirited expression
of their faith and
learning."

*Jack Ohle (2002),
launching Wartburg's
sesquicentennial year*

I am tremendously
enthusiastic and
humbled by the
opportunity of
working with an
institution that has
its foundation
rooted in faith
and service.

*Opera star Simon Estes
(2002) on his
appointment to the
Wartburg faculty*

million bond issue to get the projects under way –
and to refinance some existing debt. Results were
almost instantaneous. Walston-Hoover Stadium
was part of an outdoor athletic facilities project
completed in 2001. A maintenance building
opened in 2002, and in that same year, the campus
was turned nearly upside down by massive
construction projects related to science, the
Student Union, and the new campus entrance.

Not all changes of the early Ohle years were
visible simply by walking across the campus. Each
year brought a new record in enrollment. The
board of regents was strengthened and reorganized.
New campus information and communication
systems were put into place. The faculty developed
and adopted a new program of "Essential Education."
A major in engineering science was added; a major
in theater was restored to the curriculum after a
quarter-century absence. New faculty and adminis-

trative positions were created; record numbers
of faculty reached the age of retirement. Especially
significant was the signing in 1999 of an agreement
of cooperation with the Wartburg Castle that
encourages cultural exchanges and visits, study
opportunities and internships, and annual choir
and band performances in the castle.

Some members of the Wartburg community
who had, in Ohle's words, "spent their lives trying
to do much with little" found the pace and scale
of change almost intoxicating; for others it was
more than a little disconcerting. Wartburg was
doing some big things in a big way. It was doing
a multitude of things the right way. Faithful to
its heritage, embracing new ideas, risking new
possibilities—Wartburg College was moving to
"new levels of excellence" in its relentless quest
to give life—new life—to its calling.

Science Center Addition and Renovation
A project to more than double facilities for science began in 2002 with construction of an addition to provide new auditoriums and laboratories, followed by renovation of Becker Hall of Science classrooms, offices, and laboratories.

Athletic Complex
A 4,000-seat stadium opened in 2001 as part of a project that included a lighted football field and all-weather track in the stadium complex, plus two new soccer fields and a throwing venue for track and field on the northwest corner of the campus.

Student Union Addition and Renovation
Construction began in 2002 on expansion and renovation of the Student Union. The project also involved constructing a new multipurpose performance space and developing a new campus entrance.

CHAPTER SEVEN

Other Places, Other Times

The Wartburg tradition has come to embrace four other institutions, each of which disappeared before the middle of the twentieth century, each of which has often been described as "merging" with Wartburg College. Strictly speaking, only Eureka was merged—and in that case with St. Paul-Luther in 1933. Martin Luther Academy (Sterling), Hebron Junior College, and St. Paul-Luther College were closed, not merged. In each case, however, records were transferred, students were encouraged to do the same, and positions were offered to one or more faculty members of the closed campus. Efforts to encourage alumni and friends to identify with a new *alma mater* met with mixed results. Some quickly made the shift; others preferred to live with their memories.

The Eureka "family" gathers on campus.

Martin Luther
Academy

Martin Luther Academy
Sterling, Nebraska

Martin Luther Academy was established in 1909 by the Western District of the Iowa Synod. Located in Sterling, Nebraska, it was intended to "prepare students for entrance into the institutions at Dubuque, Clinton, and Waverly, but shall give the sons and daughters of our manses and congregations an opportunity to receive a better education than is furnished by the ordinary schools." As an academy, it offered elementary and secondary education in a coeducational, residential setting. In addition, it included a proseminary program to prepare young men for "practical" theological studies at the seminary.

Sterling never attracted many students. Closed during World War I, it was reopened following the war by the Iowa Synod in an effort to increase transfer enrollment at Clinton. Once again, students were conspicuous mostly by their absence. For several years Sterling Academy (as it was often called) "lingered between hope and despair"; in 1924 the synod decided to close it down. Male students were encouraged to continue their studies at Clinton; a handful of female students were granted a "round-trip transportation subsidy" as encouragement to attend Wartburg Normal in Waverly. Also leaving was a teacher destined for greatness on the Waverly campus—Gerhard Ottersberg.

Eureka Lutheran College
Eureka, South Dakota

Some of the same impulses that led the Western District of the Iowa Synod to create Sterling Academy in 1909 led the Dakota District to open Eureka Lutheran the following year in Eureka, South Dakota. Eureka, too, was a coeducational academy and proseminary. Like Sterling, it spent its early years in a frantic struggle to survive as a regional school. Enrollment was always uncertain. Finances were perennially desperate. At one point, each member of the faculty, including the director, was teaching no fewer than 31 classroom hours per week.

In 1917, the Iowa Synod agreed to take over Eureka. Under the leadership of George Sandrock, it was gradually transformed into a junior college— a kind of Dakota variant of Wartburg Normal

College. But not for long. The onset of the Great Depression made it abundantly clear that the new American Lutheran Church would be unable to support all of its colleges. Eureka's location, size, and grave financial condition made it particularly vulnerable. In 1933 it was merged in St. Paul with St. Paul-Luther College—which, in turn, was closed in 1935 in favor of Wartburg College in Waverly.

During its few brief years of life, Eureka Lutheran left its mark—on more than 1,500 young men and women, on a faculty that included future Wartburg stalwarts Edward Braulick, Martin Wiederaenders, Wilhelm Rodemann, and Herman Kuhlmann—and on the Eureka community and area. For a time, the college building came to be used as a Lutheran Home. Eventually abandoned to the elements, it was finally—and sadly—destroyed in the year 2000 by means of a controlled burn.

Eureka basketball
team, 1921

Eureka orchestra,
1917

Hebron College and Academy
Hebron, Nebraska

Buehring Hall,
Hebron

Responding to a heady mix of regional enthusiasm
and local booster spirit, the Ohio Synod in 1910
authorized creation of an academy in Hebron,
Nebraska. A year later, Hebron Academy opened
its doors with fifty-six students and two teachers.
Hebron developed much more solidly than either
Sterling or Eureka. In the mid-twenties it added
college-level courses and was soon accredited as
a junior college: Hebron College and Academy.

Hebron survived the consolidation efforts of
the American Lutheran Church during the 1930s,
but by the end of the decade things were no longer
going so well. A decision in 1939 to discontinue
the academy and concentrate on the college bought
only a little time. Enrollment continued to decline;
by the early months of World War II, it was no
longer feasible to keep the doors open. Hebron
was closed in 1942; its students were encouraged
to transfer to Wartburg (as many on their own
had done in the past); two members of the Hebron
faculty subsequently came to Waverly. In 1960
Wartburg honored the memory of Hebron by
placing its name on a new residence hall.

St. Paul-Luther College
St. Paul, Minnesota

St. Paul-Luther had its beginnings in the decision of an Ohio Synod pastor, H. Peter Duborg, to purchase an abandoned academy property in Afton, Minnesota, in the hope that the synod would be willing to use it as a theological seminary. The Ohio Synod agreed to do so; in 1884 it arranged to move its practical seminary program from Columbus, Ohio, to Afton. Classes at the "German Practical Theological Seminary" began in January 1885 with six students and two faculty members—one of whom was Henry Ernst, a gifted teacher and administrator who was to serve the seminary for the rest of his life (including more than thirty years as president).

The seminary program was initially two years in length; three years of preparatory work were available in the "proseminary." Within a few years, the little campus in Afton was bursting at the seams; in 1893 the seminary was moved to a magnificent new setting on the shores of Lake Phalen in St. Paul.

An increase in the number of students whose interests were not theological led to a substantial expansion of the campus—and of the curriculum. Eventually, St. Paul-Luther (as it came to be called in 1927) consisted of three departments: an academy, a two-year college, and a three-year seminary. Coeducation arrived in 1927.

Despite the vigorous leadership of President William F. Schmidt, St. Paul-Luther was not spared the trauma of the 1930s. A serious loss came in 1932, when the seminary was consolidated with Wartburg Seminary in Dubuque. In response,

William F. Schmidt, president of St. Paul-Luther College, later served as pastor of St. Paul's Lutheran Church in Waverly.

Henry Ernst served as president of St. Paul–Luther for more than thirty years.

Schmidt "reconstructed" the college by creating a four-year junior college program, embracing the final two years of high school and the first two years of college. The new program, unfortunately, was no more attractive to students than the old had been.

Similarly, the merger with Eureka in 1933 brought to St. Paul more heartache than students. The board of regents, president, and faculty were required to resign and seek reappointment; the

church appointed a new board of regents whose only qualification, in the words of President Schmidt, "was that they were ignorant of St. Paul-Luther College and uninterested in the school." Schmidt was reappointed, but conflict with the new board led him to resign in early 1934. He was replaced by Jacob Cornils, a veteran member of the faculty and college business manager. With enrollment continuing to decline, with college finances looking ever more grim, and with the outlook for the future "none too encouraging," St. Paul-Luther's only prospects lay in its attractive location. Perhaps it might become the site of a consolidated midwestern college of the church. Those hopes, faint at best, were dashed by the decision of the American Lutheran Church to close down the St. Paul campus in 1935 in favor of a "new" Wartburg College in Waverly. For many alumni and friends of St. Paul-Luther, all that was left were memories, both sweet and bitter. Some were consoled—at least a bit—by the

(top) The St. Paul-Luther campus community in 1928 included Jacob Cornils and William F. Schmidt *(front row)*

(left) The St. Paul-Luther campus was located on the shores of Lake Phalen in St. Paul, Minnesota.

courtesy: Afton Historical Society

realization that fragments of the St. Paul-Luther spirit would live on in Waverly. College records and library holdings were transferred; four members of the St. Paul-Luther faculty—John Chellevold, Jacob Cornils, Herman Kuhlmann, and Carl Muench—were invited to continue their careers at Wartburg; eighteen students made the move to Iowa; Wartburg adopted the St. Paul-Luther loyalty song as its own; William F. Schmidt spent the later years of his career as pastor of St. Paul's

congregation in Waverly and as friend and confidant of C. H. Becker. Special recognition of the St. Paul-Luther contribution to the Wartburg tradition came in 1967, when a new student housing complex was named Afton manor, and the individual units received the names of four St. Paul-Luther greats, three of whom had Wartburg College connections as well: Ernst, Schmidt, Cornils, and Chellevold.

Jacob Cornils, acting president of St. Paul-Luther at the time of its closing, continued his career as a Wartburg faculty member.

John Chellevold came to Wartburg from St. Paul-Luther in 1935 and served as professor of mathematics, academic dean, and vice-president.

Presidential Gallery

Georg Grossmann

Saginaw, 1852-1853

Dubuque, 1853-1857

St. Sebald, 1857-1868

Andrew, 1878-1879

Waverly, 1879-1894

John Klindworth

Galena, 1868-1875

Sigmund Fritschel

Mendota, 1875-1885

Friedrich Richter

Clinton, 1894-1899

Gerhard Bergstraesser

Waverly, 1905-1909

August Engelbrecht

Waverly, 1909-1933

Edward Braulick

Waverly, 1935-1945

Conrad Becker

Waverly, 1945-1964

Otto Kraushaar

Clinton, 1899-1907

John Fritschel

Clinton, 1907-1919

Otto Proehl

Clinton, 1919-1935

Friedrich Lutz

Waverly, 1894-1905

John Bachman

Waverly, 1964-1974

William Jellema

Waverly, 1974-1980

Robert Vogel

Waverly, 1980-1998

Jack Ohle

Waverly, 1998-

Faculty and Staff

In the beginning, it was Georg Grossmann and five students. Grossmann had no choice but to do it all: organize, build, administer, defend, relocate—and teach. The creation of the Iowa Synod in 1854 led gradually to the creation of multiple layers of organization. For the next century (until 1960), it was the synod that owned and operated the college, and which ultimately made the major—and sometimes not-so-major—decisions. Beginning with St. Sebald, boards of trustees were created to manage property and to keep an eye on finances and student behavior. Presidents (often with the title director) were placed in charge; ordinarily they also did some teaching. In the early twentieth century, the church created a

Board of Regents and Faculty of Wartburg College, Waverly, 1893: H. Kuhlmann, A. Bartels, J. Fritschel, F. Zimmermann, F. Schack *(top row)*; O. Kraushaar, P. Bredow, G. Grossmann, J. Deindörfer, A. Engelbrecht *(bottom row)*

Board for Christian Higher Education to coordinate and supervise its educational institutions.

In this complicated and constantly evolving set of arrangements, little interest was demonstrated in separating teaching from administration—in part, of course, because of limited resources. To teach was to administer; the reverse was equally true. Not until the second half of the twentieth century did presidents give up classroom teaching. The transformation of the faculty into a faculty of teachers occurred about the same time.

Until then, faculty held forth not only in the classroom and in curricular matters; most carried a heavy burden of administrative responsibilities as well. One usually served as college treasurer; another was assigned duties as *Hausvater*. In the early twentieth century, creation of new titles in Waverly and Clinton meant specific new assignments: dean, librarian, registrar, coach. Women teaching home economics were expected to supervise the college food service. And so it went.

In addition, faculties were expected to regulate student behavior. Students received grades in deportment until well into the twentieth century; professors kept their eyes open to student conduct both on and off the campus. While minor disciplinary matters were often handled by the *Hausvater*—or in later days by a dean—more serious offenses were referred to a faculty committee or the faculty as a whole.

With nearly every faculty member carrying some administrative duties, faculties became accustomed to an active role in the day-to-day management of the college. During the Braulick years, for instance, almost everything was referred to a faculty committee. A review of Wartburg College by the North Central Association in 1948 was critical of the faculty for spending "a rather large proportion" of its time on "administrative matters, which might have been decided by administrative officers." Presidents often were eager to get controversial matters off their desks; faculty members sometimes returned the favor. During the mid-1950s, the faculty kept its distance from the volatile issue of social dancing on campus. When the decision finally was made, C. H. Becker got the credit—and took the heat.

More than anything else, it was the demands of accreditation that moved the college toward professionalism in both faculty and staff. As early as the 1920s, state and junior college accrediting agencies were insisting on a master's degree as minimum qualification for faculty. The dream of North Central accreditation (finally realized in 1948) meant affirming academic freedom, developing a solid system of tenure, improving faculty

It is more than embarrassing to have outside speakers ask me after a convocation: Where is your faculty?

Faculty member John Hiltner (1944)

Faculty and staff in 1951.

teaching loads and salaries, increasing the numbers of faculty holding the Ph.D., providing for faculty development, and shifting faculty priorities away from administrative nitty-gritty. Membership in the American Association of University Women (AAUW) came only after Wartburg began in the late 1950s to promote women beyond the rank of Assistant Professor and to elect women to the Committee on Appointment and Rank.

Each president in the past half-century has made a commitment to strengthen the faculty. Each has been successful—in part because of increasing financial resources. President Robert Vogel, for instance, secured permanent endowments for seven faculty chairs and four professorships. Even more important has been the continuing creativity and commitment of the faculty itself. Despite inevitable tensions, shared governance is alive and well at Wartburg. The results are apparent. In its sesquicentennial year, Wartburg undoubtedly has the most gifted and effective faculty in the history of the college—with the possible exception of those early days when Georg Grossmann was teaching all by himself.

It is not yet, however, a diverse faculty. A college that for so much of its history offered education by German Lutheran men for younger German Lutheran men was terribly slow to recognize that truth and understanding might be found in other places and in other persons. The first woman to be invited to join the faculty in Waverly, Henriette Pribnow, arrived in 1914. In Clinton, Merle Gibbs accompanied the introduction of coeducation in 1928; a year later the number of women on the Clinton faculty was six. Even as their numbers have gradually increased over the years, women have had to live with persistent discrimination—in assignments, in salaries, in

> I detected [at Wartburg College] a faculty with professional aims overriding a liberal spirit.
>
> *Consultant Robert Blackburn (1969)*

Margaret Wolff Garland created a distinguished program in journalism.

promotion, in respect. Their status has improved greatly over the past half-century; much more will be required before it can be said the day of full equality has arrived.

Despite the obstacles, faculty women have contributed more than their share to the academic reputation of the college. In particular, some have been great program builders. Despite having to begin with neither space nor resources, Helen Wright established in Waverly a flourishing department of art. During the 1950s and 1960s, Margaret Wolff Garland created at Wartburg the most distinguished small-college journalism program in America. Whether measured by a never-ending flow of annual awards or by the accomplishments of alumni, or by recent shifts toward electronic media, journalism (now communication arts) has been one of Wartburg's great success stories. A contemporary of Garland, Lola Reppert, was the first great builder of Wartburg's program in social work. More recently, Carol Culton has developed an outstanding program in music therapy.

> Dr. Wiederaenders attempted to point out what it is that gives the possessor of a Ph.D. degree standing and prestige...He aroused some resentment by questioning the advisability of women aspiring to this degree.
>
> *Faculty minutes (1947)*

For all its strengths, Wartburg has not been a very attractive place for persons of color. A faculty couple from the Philippines, Edilberto and Edith Tiempo, taught briefly during the 1950s and '60s; two African-Americans, Ruth Anderson and Eric Timmer, joined the faculty in 1967. Since that time, efforts to recruit persons of color have been persistent, but not particularly successful. A few have been willing to come to Waverly; most have been unwilling to stay for very long. One notable exception was Mannie Holmes, an African-American alumnus who returned in the 1990s to teach social work, and who served as an "incredible inspiration" to Wartburg students until his untimely death in 1999.

Given the constraints of time and place, it is surprising that Wartburg faculties over the years have been blessed with so many "bright and shining stars." For the first seventy-five years, almost all the talent came from within the tradition. Few, however, could claim much by way of academic credentials. Grossmann, to be sure, had studied at Erlangen; Gottfried Fritschel

briefly had done the same. But he and his brother Sigmund, for all their intellectual brilliance, were essentially products of Löhe's mission school at Neuendettelsau. Friedrich Lutz was educated for the ministry; August Engelbrecht joined the faculty after a few years of teaching parochial school. Otto Kraushaar, whose greatness as a

Gerhard Ottersberg, great teacher, faculty leader, and college historian, was the grandson of Sigmund Fritschel.

teacher matched that of his presidency, was trained in the law. G. J. Neumann's doctorate was honorary; August Baetke, who opened the minds of so many Wartburg students, had a master's degree. Erna Moehl came to Wartburg with a master's degree and years of experience as a high school English teacher. So did Margaret Wolff Garland.

Not everyone, of course, lacked academic credentials. Alfred Haefner, Elmer Hertel, Gerhard Ottersberg, Karl Schmidt, and A. W. Swensen—Ph.D.s all—make most lists of great Wartburg teachers. So also does Herman Diers. Martin Wiederaenders deserves special recognition for leading Clinton into the world of the liberal

Mannie Holmes returned to his *alma mater* and became an "incredible inspiration" to Wartburg students. The Cultural Diversity Center bears his name.

Erna Moehl, remembered as one of Wartburg's greatest teachers, was a granddaughter of Sigmund Fritschel.

but each has found herself committed to full-time responsibilities as the spouse of a president–entertaining, hosting, operating a kind of bed-and-breakfast, comforting the sick, assisting the needy, counseling students, volunteering in the community, even grading exams. This service has gone uncompensated; for the most part, it has also been unrecognized. In 1961, however, Louise Becker was named Iowa Mother of the Year–partly because of her contributions to the life of the college. And more recently Sally Vogel has been recognized in the naming of the new library.

Faculty spouses, too, have been magnificent volunteers. Over the years, they have assisted with special events, cleaned and prepared student rooms and classrooms, opened their homes to

arts; Melvin Kramer for creating and building an outstanding program in business administration; K. D. Briner for superb leadership of Chrysalis; Robert Dell for his insistently prophetic voice. Of course there have been others. And there are others today.

A number of faculty have distinguished themselves not only by the excellence but also by the duration of their service to the college (including predecessor institutions such as Sterling and Eureka). Four of them–John Fritschel, G. J. Neumann, Ernest Heist, and Gerhard Ottersberg–each served for a half-century or more. A number of others–August Engelbrecht, A. W. Swensen, Alfred Haefner, Elmer Hertel, Martin Wiederaenders, Melvin Kramer, Warren Schmidt, William Waltmann, and David Hampton–have been members of the faculty for at least forty years.

The long tradition of presidential spouses serving as unpaid members of the staff began with Nanny Grossmann. Possibly in Saginaw, certainly in Dubuque, she was in charge of the kitchen. None of her successors has carried this burden;

Martin Wiederaenders was a prophet of the liberal arts and builder of teacher education.

students, and responded to needs wherever they have found them. When the college returned to Waverly in 1935, some of the women began meeting regularly to share food and insure that every family had enough to eat. About the same time, they began the creation of the Wartburg

Women's Club to provide social and educational opportunities for faculty, faculty wives, and other women connected to the college. Before long, the group was adding projects—some designed to improve the campus, others to assist students

Earnest Oppermann served as dean of students for a quarter-century, and also coached baseball, basketball, and football.

With a single maid, she took care of the house-keeping, meals, wash and garden. ...During the day she worked to the point of exhaustion, and at night she would sit down to do the wash and mend the clothing of the seminarians.

Sigmund Fritschel (1893), remembering Auguste von Schwartz

financially. Each year since 1959 the club has contracted with parents to bake cakes and cookies for students; the substantial proceeds are used to fund student scholarships.

Unless one counts Grossmann's maid, the beginnings of the Wartburg staff came with the arrival in Dubuque of several deaconesses sent by Löhe to assist in the seminary household. The experiment was short-lived; the deaconesses preferred to become seminary brides.

At St. Sebald, the seminary farm was placed in the hands of a manager—a position that was gradually transformed by a shift to custodial duties. And it was to St. Sebald that the sainted Auguste von Schwartz came in 1861 from St. Petersburg, Russia. She had learned about Wartburg from Sigmund Fritschel during his

fund-raising journey through Europe. Despite his warnings as to what she would find, she decided to come and serve the students as *Hausmutter*. This position was discontinued in Galena and not revived until the twentieth century—when Wartburg in Waverly became coeducational. Anna Vollmer was the first housemother of Wartburg Hall; for thirteen years (1910-1923) she was "like a mother to all." A quarter-century later, Vollmer's memory was honored when a new residence hall was dedicated as "Vollmer Hall."

Anna Vollmer, first housemother of Wartburg Hall, "Was like a mother to all."

She was the first and, for another half-century, the only woman for whom a campus building was named.

The position of *Hausvater*—and later dean of men—continued to be handled by a member of the faculty until after World War II. The same was true of most other administrative positions. Presidents typically functioned as college business managers. In 1935 Wartburg did appoint a full-time "Field and Publicity Agent" with responsibilities in public relations, alumni, admissions, student employment, and financial aid. But the move to full-time administrators came during the Becker years. Becker organized and reorganized the administrative staff and converted one responsibility after another into full-time positions: business manager, dean of the faculty, dean of students, director of development, registrar, admissions, bookstore.

Walter Fredrick, Jr.
was an astute manager of college resources during four presidencies.

Much of the dissatisfaction among women students could be traced to the fact that Wartburg does not have a dean of women.

Faculty minutes (1944)

Most of the positions most of the time were filled from within—in Becker's words, "from the Wartburg family." Becker's choices were strong ones: Alfred Haefner and John Chellevold as academic deans; Earnest Oppermann as dean of students, Merritt Bomhoff in development, Norman Fintel and Robert Gremmels in alumni and public relations, Harold Becker in church relations, Marion Fruehling in the bookstore. As chief business officer to four presidents, Walter Fredrick, Jr. came to be recognized as one of the most able administrators—regardless of position—in the history of the college. Duane Schroeder, another Becker appointee, served for forty-two years as director of public and sports information.

Dorothy Diers
was always educating, always assisting, always caring.

During the past half-century, the administrative staff has continued to grow—sometimes by the proverbial leaps and bounds. So has the support staff. Early in the century it consisted of little more than a man in charge of buildings and grounds and several women in charge of the kitchen. Secretaries first appeared in the office of the president; soon the treasurer was provided with an assistant, as was the registrar's office. And then, slowly but inexorably, all the rest. Growth of the college has been the engine of change; along with it has come a campus community of increasing complexity and rising expectations.

What has not changed is the spirit of the enterprise. Wartburg staff members are as committed to students as faculty. Often, they develop relationships with students that enable them to serve as educators. When graduates draw up lists of persons from the Wartburg community who have made a difference in their lives, they are altogether likely to include someone like Charlie Pichelmeyer or Dorothy Diers—or perhaps another one of the hundreds of staff members who have served so well for so long.

The engagement of Mrs. Ed Harden as secretary to the Director of Public Relations...is approved...but the Board as a rule does not favor the hiring of married women.

Board of Regents minutes (1941)

CHAPTER TEN

Students

He who enters places himself under the rules and discipline of the house and the ministerial influence and guidance of the teachers of the seminary, and must consent to dismissal if he makes trouble through unchristian and immoral conduct and remains impenitent.

St. Sebald (1864)

The discipline was quite strict and strictly enforced... The enforcement of the discipline, however, was handled in a spiritual and evangelical manner, so that its severity was not felt as a burden, but as a matter of course for a Christian institution, and everybody submitted willingly to it.

Mendota (1870s)

> Individual students caused us much sorrow. During the first semester one student left, disliking study, and one was dismissed as morally unfit. Similar experiences were not lacking in the second semester.
>
> *Galena (1869)*

The campus was enclosed by a barbed wire fence, protecting it against undesirable trespassers.

Waverly (1880s)

We had no privacy. Our whole freshman class studied, lived, rested, played, and existed in the room on the southwest corner of the first floor of [Old Main]. Oil lamps were used for lights, in pairs in four chandeliers, and we had to clean and fill them ourselves. A round oak stove in the corner was heated with maple wood in the fall and hard coal in winter, and we had to saw and split the wood and carry the coal and ashes in and out.

Waverly (1890s)

There was a crudely constructed washroom in the basement [of Old Main], but everybody had to furnish his own washbasin. Calls of nature had to be answered in a six-section outhouse, which stood some distance away from the building.

Waverly (1890s)

All our complaints to the director of the college did not improve our daily bread. The food was not the best quality and I remember being served fish that had a bad odor. The students became rebellious. The director told us he would not listen to our complaints. Then the whole student body began to stomp on the wooden floor. The director walked out, the students following him in order to storm his office, but he had locked the door. The result was that glass pitchers were bought to serve molasses, and fish eliminated from the menu, but the diet was not improved.

Clinton (1890s)

Several other German students and I have a special friendship, and we try to hold our own with the American students. There is constant friction. The students like to put down the Germans, but my German heritage doesn't stand for that. I am happy here, there are many opportunities, but it is not a land of milk and honey.

Clinton (1899)

In the four years I spent at Wartburg, I never got to town, met no people except at church. No one except my class-mates knew that I never owned an overcoat while in school.

Waverly (1890s)

May Day in
Waverly (1919)

Resolved to move the library into the NE room on the third floor [of Old Main], room to be locked and [a student] appointed to issue books at stated periods to those desiring them.

Waverly (1907)

> "Shagging"–hazing of freshmen––was a popular custom. I could not see how this practice, so demeaning to human dignity, fitted very well into a Christian school.
>
> *Clinton (1908)*

Wartburg was virtually a "German island in the English sea." There was little contact between the school and the outside world–and no coeducation. The administration didn't look kindly on students associating with women. It was almost a monastic life.

Clinton (1910)

Sneaking off to town . . . was not uncommon. If detected it would lead to several weeks of campus arrest. Smoking was permitted only after students had passed their 18th birthday (most of them still entered at 14) and then only with written consent of the parents and even then cigarettes were strictly forbidden. Movies were just becoming common; silent flickers known as nickel-shows were not forbidden, but frequent or habitual attendance was frowned upon. A legitimate theater existed in the city. It was ordinarily out of bounds, but general permission to attend was granted when, e.g., a Shakespearean troupe appeared. There was also a vaudeville show in the city which was unconditionally taboo, but which had fairly regular visitors who felt reasonably safe, because the faculty could not well attend and catch them. Slipping into a saloon to sip a beer was a heinosus act likely to lead to dismissal, but there were reprobate characters who did that too.

Clinton (1915)

We had what seems in retrospect a plethora of activities: orchestra, band, glee clubs, mixed chorus, a debating team (briefly), declamatory contests, a Lutheran Brotherhood club, a student monthly newspaper, a year-book, a dramatic society, literary societies (everyone was expected to choose one of the three such), and, of course the class organizations. Only in athletics and physical education were we short-changed.

Waverly (1918)

Discipline was unusually difficult during this year. An evil, unchristianlike spirit prevailed among the students, and the faculty saw themselves more than once forced to vigorously move in and inflict severe punishment on some of the students.

Clinton (1919)

Although girls and boys met in classes daily, we were forbidden to fraternize in any way beyond the structured meetings of the approved school organizations. Dating a girl was a risky business, accomplished usually by Sunday afternoon walks along the railroad tracks.

Waverly (1918)

[During the influenza epidemic of 1918] the entire student body had to be quarantined . . . which meant that we could not leave the campus, whatever the reason. . . . Four of the thirty boys in my sleeping quarters died of the dreaded disease. Those of us who survived kept wondering who would be next.

Waverly (1918)

Our sleeping quarters were crowded into a dormered attic room, while all the toilet and bathing facilities were concentrated in one large room in the basement. So if one had to respond to nature's call at night, you had to make your way along a dimly lit corridor and descend three sets of drafty staircases.

Clinton (1920s)

On weekends we made forays into the countryside, sometimes pilfering grapes, apples, peaches, watermelons, or strawberries in season; or we rented canoes and explored the shoreline and some of the islands of the Mississippi River. Most of us went to Clinton by trolley Sunday mornings to attend services at Zion Lutheran, and that led occasionally to an invitation to dinner and an introduction to a daughter and some of her friends.

Clinton (1920s)

Play cast, Clinton, 1918: Gerhard Ottersberg (*fifth from right*); August Baetke (*third from right*)

It was plain that in the absence of women the table manners of young men all but vanished.
Clinton (1920s)

The pattern of social and extracurricular life at the two institutions [Waverly and Clinton] differed markedly. At Clinton there was much less talk about girls and dating, while the extracurricular attention centered on athletics–chiefly baseball and basketball–the orchestra, and the literary societies.

Clinton/Waverly (1920s)

> A dramatic group on campus produced at least one play annually in the downtown Clinton Theatre. In the absence of coeds, males were cast in women's roles, with predictably hilarious outcomes.
>
> *Clinton (1920s)*

In order to promote economy and prevent a feeling of inequality among lady students, the school management urges simplicity of dress in general. For school and classroom wear, such goods as georgette crepe, silk, and velvet are not approved by the faculty.

Waverly (1923)

Complaints about the meals may be registered with the student senior or directly with the president. In no instance may reference to the matter be made to those in charge of the kitchen.

Clinton (1927)

Making their inspection rounds in Grossmann Hall the members of the Visiting Committee found that the rooms of some of the students presented a spectacle of disorder and untidiness, and that cleanliness which is next to godliness was conspicuously absent.

Waverly (1927)

It is true that the campus life of Wartburg is shy of some things found in other schools. But Clinton strives to give your sons an education with the monkey business omitted.

Clinton (1928)

In 1929 coeducation was in its second year, so those of the female persuasion could act coy before accepting an offer of a date, which included a streetcar ride to a movie and ice cream parlor.

Clinton (1929)

Resolved . . . that brief Chapel talks, based on a word of scripture (no long-winded exhortations) not to exceed 5-8 minutes in length, be given by the teachers appointed by the director.

Waverly (1931)

Another old tradition is the annual Leaf-raking Day, which also proves to be more or less of a picnic, at least for the girls.

Waverly (1929)

It was reported that there had been a great deal of criticism of the dance by Miss Miller during the pageant at the close of the school year. Director Engelbrecht stated that he would see to it that no such dance would again be performed. Mr. Ottersberg took the liberty to state that he had not thought the dance obscene. This view was sharply rebuked.

Waverly (1931)

Professor Swensen, who acted as chairman of the [student mixer] program committee, asked the boys and girls to form two lines. Then he took all the boys and girls for a walk. Evidently their idea was that if some of the students were bashful, they would overcome that by walking and in time they would say something.

Waverly (1931)

Since the Northern Illinois Conference will meet in Wartburg College on April 21-22, it was decided to set up beds in the attic of the Main Building. The students living in the south unit of Cotta House are to move to the attic of the Main building during this time so that conference guests may have the use of Cotta House.

Clinton (1931)

Students are requested to refrain from throwing refuse out of the windows.

Clinton (1931)

Stacks in the library are now closed to keep order, to keep persons out, and to help make fortnightly papers more creative.

St. Paul-Luther (1933)

Intellectually [the male students] are rather numb and show very little curiosity. . . . [They] find the town too small, especially on weekends. Many of them have no cash for entertainment–hence lie around. The weekend situation is serious. Some form of recreation must be found for them.

Waverly (1935)

Girl students are rooming in the homes of the professors. These rooms have been requisitioned by the institution and the professors do not receive any remuneration for room rent.

Clinton (1933)

Stacked boots

Dr. Haefner remarked that so many pre-theological students are on academic probation and so few on the honor roll.

Waverly (1936)

Wartburg is free from the rivalry, the narrowness, and the extravagance usually connected with the fraternity and sorority system. At Wartburg all students live together in one friendly democratic relationship which welds them together into one loyal unit. They learn to rub shoulders with others, to understand, to appreciate various viewpoints, learn the art of living together, cooperating together, playing together. There they acquire the proper social graces; here they also learn the first principles of self-government, of self-reliance, and of personal responsibility, altogether a wonderful educational experience in living.

Waverly (1936)

> Students are not permitted to take girls out riding after dark.
> *Waverly (1936)*

It seems desirable that the school rent some acreage in order to procure its own garden supplies for the ensuing school year 1936-37. We have sufficient "student labor" to man forty or more acres of tillable soil. We also have barn space for four or more milk cows. It would be profitable for us to purchase a number of cows and to assign students to their care.

Waverly (1936)

All girls, except those living with relatives, shall be required to fill out a blank each week and return it to Mrs. LaBahn. On this blank the girls will indicate how they spend their time outside school hours.

Waverly (1940)

Homecoming
theme: "War
Maneuvers"
Wartburg Hall:
"No Man's Land"
Banquet menu:
"Cannon balls,
bomb shells,
shrapnel,
nitroglycerine"

Waverly (1940)

The complaint was made that too many students have no free evenings, or at least very few for study; that their time is taken up by extra-curricular activities.

Waverly (1938)

Professor Swensen reported on the work of the Committee on Business Management. He spoke of the activities of the staff of the *Fortress* and the staff of the *Trumpet,* and stressed the thought that the sponsors of various activities are personally responsible if their organizations become involved in debt.

Waverly (1942)

> Wartburg students did not like to wear their initiation beanies off-campus. Waverly kids poked fun at them; calling them "Krauts."
> *Waverly (1940s)*

(left) Freshmen
hold their
beanies as they
"button" to
upperclassmen,
a ritual of
initiation.

The girls had a sore grievance. They were supposed to be in their dormitory rooms by 8:30 every weekday evening and by 10:30 on weekends, while there were no rules for boys. This gave rise to the intolerable situation that boys could have two dates on one evening—one with their college sweetheart and one with a high school lass or some other girl uptown.

Waverly (1940s)

Wartburg was loaded with GIs so I quickly got involved with student government, which the vets thought needed overhauling. The vets were not going to put up with much of the rule-making and enforcement and, of course, felt the 18-21-year-olds weren't dry behind the ears.

Waverly (1948)

Students who do not believe in our religious program are out of place here, and we will ask them to make room for others who are eager to have the opportunity to attend a Christian college.

Waverly (1948)

Women students were still referred to as girls and had to be in their dorm room early every evening except on the weekends–which weren't much more liberal. Dancing was strictly forbidden, as was alcohol in the dorms. Few students had cars, which meant that most of us had to walk if we wanted to go to downtown Waverly.

Waverly (1951)

I had been elected to be the editor of the next year's *Trumpet* and wanted to issue a summer paper called the *Hot Trumpet.* The administration determined that such a name was just too "jazzy," so we had to call it the *Trumpette.*

Waverly (1951)

Gentlemen may come to the dormitories to call for girls on Sunday morning, but there shall be no visiting in the lounges.

Waverly (1957)

As an undergraduate I transferred to Wartburg from a much wealthier and better-known college. In three semesters, Wartburg changed my major, my vocational plans, and my sense of values.

Waverly (1960s)

The Library
welcomes all new
and old students
for the coming
school year,
and adds in a
whisper—"SH-sh!"

Waverly (1948)

Extended living

I had been plucked from the tropics and transplanted to the middle of Iowa cornfields. The educational and cultural shock was almost too much, but with the help of roommates and close friends, I not only survived but learned to love the college and town.

Waverly (1960s)

More cruel than
initiation is the
torture of standing
in line to pay
your bills.

Waverly (1965)

[North Hall] had a reputation for drinking but probably didn't consume as much as some of the other dorms. We did have several keg parties throughout the year, and there was often a "study break" about midnight, when a group of the guys went for a beer at Maxfield's or perhaps just an egg-cheese at Roy's Place.

Waverly (1960s)

It may be that not many sedate alumni . . . can see in Wartburg's first panty raid last spring an outstanding indication of achievement.

Waverly (1967)

Upon recommendation of the deans, the cabinet took action to refuse the request of the Women's Judiciary Council "that women be allowed to wear sports clothes in the cafeteria on Friday evenings."

Waverly (1965)

By action of the president's cabinet women are to be allowed to wear slacks in the library.
Waverly (1968)

Wartburg College is a peculiar malady. You catch it by coming here, and you have it for the rest of your life. . . . You catch it not from any one factor or person, but instead from exposure to a unique combination of elements: from a close association with the faculty, from the wide variety of experiences available in the May Term, from close friendships formed with many varieties of students, from the wider opportunities for personal action.

Waverly (1960s)

Last weekend an unknown group of Wartburg students burned a "W" on Luther's football field. The following night, Luther students attempted to retaliate and were dispersed by a large group of Wartburg students. During the dispersal, two Luther students' heads were shaved and several Luther cars damaged.

Waverly (1971)

The Board of Regents has eliminated the last vestige of women's hours.

Waverly (1971)

One morning, as she was sweeping a dormitory floor, [a member of the maintenance staff] stopped to pick up a penny. A student observing her asked why she would bend down to pick up a penny. She told him that whenever she found a coin, she put it in her shoe, and every time she felt the coin, it reminded her to say a prayer for her grandson, who was very ill. The next morning, when she came to sweep that same floor, it was covered with pennies.

Waverly (1980s)

At Bethsaida, the students had time to wonder about the battleworn, biblical past of the place and to learn something too about themselves and how they fit into this history. We became so familiar with the land of Jesus that the gospel stories will never be the same.

Waverly (1980s)

Wartburg must make students aware that the ladder to success can be very narrow and confining... There is something about the Wartburg experience that leads to concern and openness. It's inspiring.

Waverly (1987)

> Denver's diversity, opportunity, and excitement helped me discover myself. Through my experiences at Wartburg West, I have a clear sense of who I am and what my dreams and goals are.
>
> *Waverly (1990)*

[On a service trip to Washington, D. C.], my encounters with homeless people, volunteers, and political leaders challenged me to question the ideas and stereotypes instilled in me as a child. My interactions with people from other cultures and backgrounds served me more than I ever could have served them.

Waverly (1990s)

...from passing the peace at Eucharist to passing the time at Joe's.

Waverly (1996)

Cleaning up

Campus Ministry

As a college committed to faith and learning, Wartburg has always made provision both for the study of religion and for the creation of a worshipping community. During the first century, the setting was coercive. Students had no choice but to register each year for courses in the faith; attendance at morning and evening devotions was mandatory. So was worship in a nearby congregation on Sunday mornings. Student discipline was administered in a "spiritual and evangelical manner."

By the time that Wartburg settled permanently in Waverly (1935), attendance at worship—evening chapel and Sunday morning services at St. Paul's—had become "semi-voluntary": expected but not required. Religious programs were, however, a regular part of the convocation program—and there attendance was still required. Students of the 1960s recall with a smile the click of "Oppie's camera," which created an incontestable record

of who was present (at the moment, at least) and who was not.

Campus life in both Clinton and Waverly included student organizations with a religious orientation: the Lutheran Brotherhood (later the Luther League), the Missionary Society, Chi Rho (for pre-seminary students), and others. These organizations tended to flourish—in part because until the 1960s nearly 90 percent of the student body was Lutheran.

In 1959, the college called Herman Diers as campus pastor with a mandate to organize a student congregation. Completion of the Chapel-Auditorium (later renamed Neumann Auditorium) in 1960 provided space, and for a few years the campus congregation flourished. But not for long. The Vietnam years spawned a youth culture which manifested little enthusiasm for traditional values and institutions. Large numbers of students lost interest in campus ministry; so did many members of the faculty; Herman Diers moved on

As to attendance [at chapel], the chairman was strongly inclined to make it compulsory and to advise non-Lutherans who would not comply to go elsewhere.

Board of Directors minutes (1931), Wartburg Normal College

My most important learning at college has come through the [campus] ministry here.

Charles Kurtz (1991) on his education at Wartburg

The good thing that has come out of this is that in my twenty-seven years here, I've never before seen 200 students ...debating what it means to be a college of the church.

College Pastor Larry Trachte (2001) on the debate over the future of Danforth Chapel

Chapel at Clinton

The Wartburg Chapel, dedicated in 1994, revitalized the worship life of the college and outreach programs of campus ministry organizations.

to Chrysalis; for several years seminary interns filled in. At one point, tiny Danforth Chapel was the site of midweek campus worship. By the time Larry Trachte was called as campus pastor in 1974, religious life was not dead, but it no longer evidenced much sense of community.

The past quarter century has seen a rebirth of ministry on campus. It is a different time; the program has benefited from Trachte's strong leadership; daily chapel has been restored; the department of religion provides effective support; in 1994 came the completion of the long-awaited Wartburg Chapel. The days of huge student faith organizations have long since passed; today, students come together in smaller, more intimate settings for study, prayer, and fellowship. Midweek Eucharist has become a moving "celebration of grace."

With non-Lutherans now constituting half the student body, the community of faith at Wartburg College is both Lutheran and ecumenical. The challenges for ministry in this setting are enormous. For some, the college has become too open in matters of faith; for others, it still is not open enough. The conversation continues. What is encouraging is the number of students—and faculty—who care deeply about it.

Outfly

Outfly is the most enduring of Wartburg traditions; it is also the most mutable. For 120 years, Outfly has forever been in the process of becoming. The strange name is a literal translation of the German *Ausflug* (excursion, outing)—which is what it was in the beginning. The first mention of *Ausflug* comes from Mendota in 1883: students went on a Friday-Saturday excursion to nearby Starved Rock, now a state park. Probably they traveled most of the way by train; possibly they were accompanied by faculty; the experience may, or may not, have been repeated in Mendota.

August Engelbrecht once recalled that the Outfly tradition in Waverly dated "from the beginning." Possibly it was brought along from Mendota when the college was moved to Waverly in 1885. Whatever the case, faculty minutes for October 5, 1892, note that *Ausflug* was scheduled for the following day.

Two years later the college was in Clinton; so was *Ausflug*. And it is in Clinton that we see the first evidence of a shift to student initiative and spontaneity: the early morning cries of *Ausflug*, the decision by the faculty to cancel classes for the day, the march to a park followed by a picnic and a variety of games and entertainments, and finally, at the end of the day, the long walk home. This same general pattern developed in Waverly as well. "Outings" came to be regular features of life on both campuses; eventually, with the shift from German to English, they came to be called "Outfly."

Over the course of a century, almost everything about Outfly has changed—often more than once. Spontaneity has given way to careful, though secretive, scheduling; authorization has moved from faculty to president. From time to time Outfly has been called once, or twice, or even three times during a year. In early Waverly,

Outfly sometimes involved a winter day of skating on the Cedar River. When Clinton became coeducational in 1928, the men followed up the usual Fall Outfly with a second outing to save themselves "from suffering too severely from the shock of transition." Transportation to and from the several "Outfly parks" came to include not only marches and hikes, bicycles, and autos, but also "taking the train" to Riverview Park on the Shell Rock River near Waverly. For some years, Outfly in Waverly included a snake dance through the city; at one time Fall Outfly marked the end of freshman initiation.

The great change in Outfly during the last half-century, however, has been the erosion of its potential for building community. Once upon a time, Outfly brought almost everyone together—faculty, staff, students—and then took them together to another place for a day of recreation and engagement. For understandable reasons, nearly all of that has been lost. Despite continuing efforts to find new ways of building connections, Outfly has become mostly a day for pursuing personal interests—either on or off the campus. In one sense, about all that has remained unchanged is the cancellation of classes. But Outfly lives. It lives despite periodic efforts to put it to sleep. It lives because it is wrapped in ritual and steeped in tradition. It lives because it belongs to nobody else. Outfly is Wartburg.

> Outfly! Not the attenuated travesty persisting today . . . but a sunny fall day or a balmy spring day joyously to be spent in the open, climbing cliffs at Eagle Point or boating on the broad Mississippi at East Lynne.
>
> *Clinton*

Faculty members serve the picnic lunch during Outfly.

Organized in columns, the students began the long march to the park. Two colleagues and I were assigned the task of keeping the marchers in line and in step. . . . We were fairly successful as the group marched through town, but after that our influence waned. American students did not relish marching in military formation, especially if the leadership was German. The closer we came to the park the less precise our marching. . . . As we approached the park, ranks broke and students spilled across the walks and lawns like waves of the sea.

Clinton (1897)

Kitten ball, horseshoe, and bicycling held charms for the more active, but most of Wartburg was content to sit and talk, or just to sit, through a golden, lazy autumn afternoon.

Waverly (1937)

[President Braulick reported] that some of the students were in favor of dispensing with Fall Outfly and having a holiday on the Friday following Thanksgiving. Though no action was taken, the faculty seemed to favor dropping the Spring Outfly rather than the Fall Outfly.

Waverly (1941)

> Everyone parties it up the night before. If Outfly isn't called the next day, Miss Mead [college nurse] has many visitors with various ailments, mostly headaches.
> *Waverly (1964)*

With utter disregard for orders issued by the administration, student leaders organized student mob action to obtain permission for an outing.

Waverly (1942)

...the Spring Outfly day began with special zest because the day promised to be warm and beautiful, but ended with the cold wind of death because two students drowned in the Cedar River.

Waverly (1966)

I was terrified. Someone was playing a bugle call and people were running and pounding on our residence hall doors. We didn't know what to expect. . . . Outfly is one of the many things that makes Wartburg special.

Waverly (1998)

Concert Halls

The educational interests of the Iowa Synod did not include the visual arts. At the turn of the century, Otto Kraushaar publicly indicated an admiration for German art, but that admiration was never translated into program. Otto Proehl, on the other hand, was not only an advocate; he lectured on art, he arranged for others to do the same, and he regularly brought art exhibits to the Clinton campus. In 1929 the college began to offer courses in art and art appreciation. All this came to an end with the closing of Clinton in 1935; the new Wartburg in Waverly waited a year before restoring art—on a limited basis—to the curriculum. It has taken half a century to develop the kind of excellence which the department can now claim.

Music, on the other hand, was central to the life of the college from the very beginning. German Lutherans found it difficult to worship without singing. Georg Grossmann never ceased being an advocate for music; his understanding of teacher education included skill development in piano and singing. When he reduced his teaching responsibilities at St. Sebald, the one area he retained was music. Friedrich Lutz was an accomplished musician, so also were Friedrich Richter and August Engelbrecht. It is not at all surprising that music became a distinguishing feature of the Wartburg experience.

In terms of curriculum, development was slow. Initially, music instruction was geared to the preparation of elementary school teachers. A music department was created in Waverly just after the turn of the century; in Clinton, similar development came with the arrival of F. E. Schoenbohm in the late 1920s. On both campuses, expanded programs were intended to serve not only the campus, but private-lesson students from the community as well. When the college was "merged" in Waverly in 1935, a department of music was included. Under the leadership of Edwin Liemohn, it grew rapidly during the 40s and 50s to become one of the college's largest departments—a status that continues to the present day.

Curriculum is part of the story. Performance is another. Here the tradition began with choral singing. We have only a few glimpses of the early years: students singing "A Mighty Fortress Is Our God" from the balcony at St. Sebald on the day of dedication; the teachers seminary chorus, directed by Georg Grossmann, singing at the dedication of Old Main in Waverly—and subsequently in area congregations as well; student August Engelbrecht being selected by conductor Friedrich Richter as soloist for the choir in Mendota. The tradition continued in both Waverly and Clinton; from time to time the structures changed. In Clinton, the introduction of coeducation resulted in a women's chorus as well as a mixed chorus. The men's chorus teamed with its counterpart from Wartburg Seminary to tour as the "Wartburg Lutheran Male Chorus." A male quartet

Wartburg College Band, Clinton, 1909

The Wartburg Normal 1,000-mile tour required more than simply playing instruments.

On our orchestra tour 1929
WE PUSHED THE BUS AHEAD
US OUT OF A MUDHOLE.

traveled through the Midwest each summer, promoting the college to prospective students and their parents.

Early in the twentieth century, Wartburg in Waverly developed both a "Boys Glee Club" and a mixed chorus. As the number of women students increased, a "Girls Glee Club" was added, but no tradition of touring developed. Conductors included persons with familiar surnames: Hilda Grossmann (granddaughter of Georg Grossmann) and Dorothy Kraushaar (daughter of Otto Kraushaar).

When the college returned to Waverly in 1935, the single appointment in music went to Ernest Heist, a veteran of Wartburg Normal days who had remained in Waverly when the school was closed in 1933. Heist organized an *a cappella* choir—the Wartburg Choir—as well as a male chorus, and reluctantly arranged for spring tours of both organizations. Two years later Heist was

replaced by Edwin Liemohn, whose enthusiasm for touring became legendary. Tours were lengthened in duration and itinerary—Canada, California, and in 1959, Europe.

Liemohn's successor, James Fritschel, took advantage of the May Term to schedule extensive European tours on a regular basis; in 1980 the Wartburg Choir won first place at the Cork International Choral Festival in Ireland. The choir's reputation for world-class excellence has continued under Paul Torkelson, an alumnus who became director in 1984. Following reunification of Germany, Torkelson has been able to build a special relationship with the Wartburg Castle. The choir has performed there regularly—the only American choir privileged to do so.

Over the years, student interest in singing has led to the creation of a variety of vocal ensembles. The Castle Singers, once the "second choir," has evolved into a jazz group which, like the choir, has

toured extensively—both in the United States and throughout the world. The Ritterchor has revived the male chorus tradition; the St. Elizabeth Chorale has done the same for women. To these have been added a Chapel Choir and a Gospel Choir.

A band was organized in Waverly in 1898; one of its stated functions was to provide music for Outfly. In Clinton the same development came three years later. Institutional support was meager; students served as directors; ordinarily they managed to recruit only a handful of players. About the time of World War I, bands began to give way to orchestras, and within a few years had disappeared from the scene.

Orchestras, too, were organized by students early in the century. A decade later they enjoyed adult leadership, and in 1918 the Clinton orchestra scheduled a tour in Wisconsin—apparently the first in college history. For years, the orchestra was the great touring organization. During the 1920s, tours also included a small glee club drawn from the personnel of the orchestra. In Waverly

the orchestra fared less well; in 1931 a student-led band once again took its place.

The reestablishment in 1935 of Wartburg in Waverly made no provision for instrumental music. Students managed to create a short-lived orchestra, a pep band, and a German band, but further progress had to await the end of the depression and World War II.

The master builder of the Wartburg College Band was Robert E. Lee. Over a period of several decades, he established a superb ensemble whose opportunities for touring came to match those of the choir and Castle Singers. More recently, conductor Craig A. Hancock has multiplied student opportunity by creating two concert bands: the Symphonic Band and the Wind Ensemble. And for years, interested students have had the opportunity of performing in the Knightliters Jazz Band, which now tours with the Castle Singers.

In the early 1950s, Ernest Hagen, director of the Wartburg College Band, became interested in reestablishing the orchestra. Only a few string

Our glee club… sang a program of very trite songs, such as "Oh, the Bulldog on the Bank, and the Bull-frog in the Pool," "Sweet Kentucky Babe," and so forth.

Otto Kraushaar, (son of President Kraushaar), (1988) on touring in the early 1920s

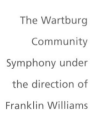

The Wartburg Community Symphony under the direction of Franklin Williams

players were available on campus, so Hagen began recruiting from Northeast Iowa, and in the process created the Wartburg Community Symphony. Waverly remains one of the smallest cities in the nation to support a symphony orchestra. Strong leadership—especially from conductors Franklin Williams and Janice Wade—has brought it to an often-thrilling level of artistic excellence. In 2002 it begins its fiftieth season.

Each Christmas, the music organizations of the college join forces in presenting a concert as a gift to the community. Begun in 1947, Christmas with Wartburg has evolved into a major and memorable event—not only on campus, but in other nearby cities to which it has been carried: Cedar Falls, Des Moines, and Cedar Rapids.

Performing organizations have taken Wartburg to the world. The world—at least some parts of it—has been brought to Wartburg by faculty and

students, but also by a steady stream of visitors, speakers, and performing artists.

In Clinton, students could journey downtown to take in an occasional Shakespearean play, band concert, or symphony performance. Waverly presented fewer such opportunities. By the early twentieth century, however, faculty and students were often attending piano and vocal recitals sponsored by the Waverly German Male Chorus at the Waverly Opera House.

Then, in 1920, the Waverly campus dedicated a gymnasium—designed to be used also as an auditorium. And in that same year Wartburg Normal College inaugurated "The Waverly Lyceum Course," presenting "Five Big Entertainments." The founder of the Lyceum was Oswald Hardwig, who a few years earlier had been instrumental in establishing the department of music. After several years at the helm, Hardwig yielded to

A.W. Swensen presided over the "glory days" of the Artist Series, built the chemistry department, coached athletics, and conducted the orchestra.

A. W. Swensen, who over the next half-century took the series from Lyceum obscurity to Artist Series glory. Along the way, there were a few misses: a lecturer in 1938 demonstrated "the first seeing-eye dog west of the Mississippi." But by mid-century Swensen was attracting the finest talent in the world: Artur Rubinstein, Jascha Heifetz, Carl Sandberg, the Robert Shaw Chorale, Charles Laughton, Marian Anderson, the Boston Pops—and a host of others. Students flocked to Artist Series concerts and lectures; so did hundreds of patrons from throughout Northeast Iowa. Sometimes Knights Gymnasium was packed with more than 3,000 listeners.

Swensen's successors managed to maintain the same high standards of excellence, but the days of attracting to Waverly the superstars of music and theatre gradually disappeared. A recent and radiant exception is opera star Simon Estes, who has twice been an Artist Series performer, and who agreed in 2002 to become a member of the Wartburg College faculty.

Augmenting the Artist Series have been a number of student-sponsored pops concerts, bringing to the campus over the years artists such as Duke Ellington, Louis Armstrong, Henry Mancini, Stan Kenton, and Dave Brubeck.

Convocations at Wartburg go back to the days of Wartburg Normal College. Scheduled once a week to bring students and faculty together for education and worship, they were sometimes devoted to meetings of the student body. Beginning in 1935, convocations were held on a daily basis; in 1948 the college shifted to 50-minute programs on Tuesdays and Thursdays—some educational, some religious. Whatever the frequency, student attendance was mandatory; faculty attendance was not. Even so, week after week, year after year, most of the campus came together on a regular basis. It was a great opportunity for community-building, and mid-century presidents and deans made the most of it.

In recent years, the frequency of convocations has been reduced to a handful each term; mandatory attendance disappeared long ago. But "convo" still brings faculty and students and the Waverly community together; it still brings people of prominence to campus. The list of outstanding speakers is long: Alan Greenspan, Arnold Toynbee, Alex Haley, Norman Borlaug, Ralph Abernathy, Dick Gregory, Elizabeth Dole, Martin Marty— and more. Some of the best have been relative unknowns. In 1970, convocation brought to campus a "pow-wow" of the American Indian Movement. Several hundred Native Americans, including Dennis Banks and Clyde Bellecourt, traveled to Waverly for a few days of engagement on the campus and in the community. For all who participated, it was the convocation of a lifetime.

Your contribution to the cultural life in central Iowa . . . is a constant reminder that dynamic programming does not have to remain in the cities.

Impresario Sol Hurok, in a retirement tribute to A. W. Swensen (1968)

CHAPTER TWELVE

Playing Fields

In its early years the educational enterprise that was to become Wartburg College was almost entirely a matter of disciplined mind and spirit. Days were filled with study and worship and prayer—and occasionally a little music. Students, to be sure, got more than their share of exercise in constructing buildings at Saginaw and St. Sebald. And in every one of the early locations there were daily chores—especially in St. Sebald, where wood needed to be cut and sawed, and where water had to be carried from a spring half a mile away. Life was a difficult,

Baseball in Clinton, 1908: G. Hanssler, S. Blessin, H. Neemann, G. Landgrebe (*fourth row*); B. Foelsch, C. Domke (*third row*); H. Kumpf, J. Vollstedt, F. Voelker, R. Huegel, W. Fruehling (*second row*); J. Burke (*first row*)

Gymnastics at
Clinton

serious business. To find joy in a required activity was one thing; to seek amusement was quite another.

The first evidence of a shift toward recreational values came in the late 1870s in Mendota. Students there began to play the American game of baseball—among themselves. A few years later, students at the new teachers seminary in Waverly were doing the same; on occasion they would challenge—usually without success—a team of "Waverlyites." Students migrating from Waverly to Clinton in 1894 undoubtedly took "ball playing" along with them; the college catalog for 1899-1900 mentions both a "baseball team" and a "football team." Several years later, however, a serious injury led to the discontinuation of competitive football. Construction of a small gymnasium at Clinton in 1907 opened the door a few years later to basketball; early in the century, student tennis associations were created at both Wartburgs.

The development of each sport in each place followed a similar pattern. Initiative came from the students, who after competing against each other were eager to challenge other nearby teams—mostly high school, sometimes independent (the "Clinton Cigar Company," the "Dixon Unions"), sometimes collegiate. Funding came entirely from student resourcefulness; so also did leadership. Participants usually selected one of their own as coach or manager; occasionally they were able to secure the volunteer services of a faculty member. Eligibility requirements were self-defined and exceedingly flexible; a young faculty member, Ernest Heist, played shortstop on the 1913 Wartburg baseball team in Waverly.

While presidents, faculties, and boards of directors paid little attention to intramural contests (except football—because of the special risk of injury), they took a keen interest in any competition that might take students off campus and away from their studies. President Otto Kraushaar in Clinton (1899-1907) was an enthusiast for physical activity and competition; his successor, John Fritschel, was not. Despite a brand-new gymnasium, it took students a half-decade of agitation to gain permission to play

He spent much of his time collecting funds for a gym— for which he was criticized by some of the parents who said they sent their boys to college to get an education, not to play ball.

Ella Kraushaar, remembering her father, Otto Kraushaar

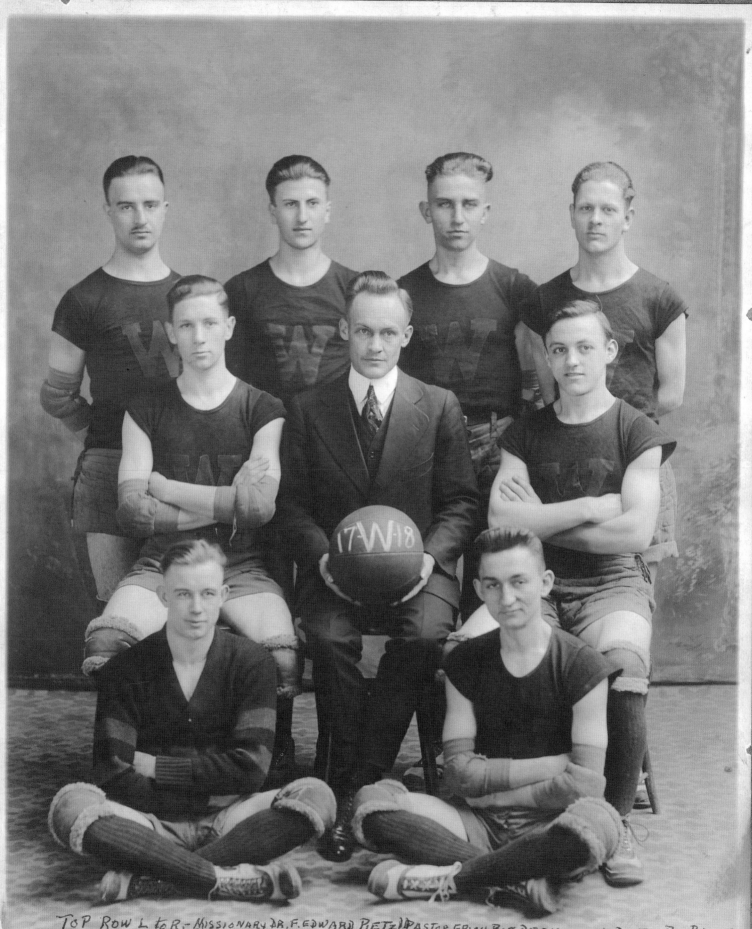

TOP ROW L to R.- MISSIONARY DR. F. EDWARD PIETZ, PASTOR ERICH BIEDERMANN (d), PASTOR PAUL RADLOFF (d)
    PASTOR AUG. SUECHTING
CENTER- HENRY FISCHER (d), COACH, PROF. MARTIN HUETER (d), DR. HERMANN W. SIEFKES, WAVERLY
FLOOR- PASTOR TRAUGOTT HERBENER, WIS.- FRANZ KUHLMANN (d)

WARTBURG COLLEGE, CLINTON, IOWA

The beginnings of football.

(left) Clinton men's basketball team, 1917-18

When the baseball season came the team started practicing, but some of the members were so engaged in our concerts that they could not find sufficient time to practice, and they met defeat twice at the hands of the Clinton High School team. This discouraged the team as well as the students and all scheduled games were cancelled, and all time devoted to music.

From the Wartburg Quarterly [Clinton] (1912)

competitive basketball. Baseball fared a little better, but for a number of years no games outside Clinton were permitted. And football, except on an intramural basis, continued to be forbidden altogether until 1929.

In Waverly the inauguration of competition in basketball had to await completion in 1920 of a gymnasium. Permission to play football came in 1922, only to be withdrawn a few years later, and then reinstated in 1928. For the first quarter of the twentieth century, baseball was *the* major sport in Waverly. In 1909 an academy student, Alexander "Rube" Schauer, pitched the team to a successful season before moving on to a five-year career in the "Big Leagues" with the New York Giants and Philadelphia Athletics. When in 1914 the baseball team requested permission to go to Clinton for a series of games, the faculty denied the request, insisting that the team play no more than the usual three games away from home.

Almost from the beginning, educators in Waverly and Clinton were interested not only in keeping athletics under control, but also in providing physical and recreational opportunities for the entire student body. Shortly after the completion in 1880 of Old Main in Waverly, parallel bars and a trapeze were installed on the campus. Otto Kraushaar, then a member of the Waverly faculty, supervised a mandatory gymnastics program. Sometimes, when the weather was favorable, he would substitute a student march to the Cedar River for bathing and swimming. When Kraushaar moved on to Clinton and became president there, his interest in a gymnasium was grounded in a desire to provide year-round facilities for gymnastics.

Coeducation at Waverly stimulated a special interest in the physical well-being of young women. In 1914 the Waverly faculty made physical exercises mandatory for all students. Implementation

Women's calisthenics

during winter months was difficult, however, until the construction of a gymnasium in 1920. Beginning in 1919, women students found ways of competing in basketball with Waverly High School, but permission for a women's basketball program awaited the arrival of Lydia Wimmer as a member of the faculty in 1923. She organized a women's basketball team and scheduled a handful of games with nearby high schools and a business college in Waterloo. The final game of the season had to be forfeited when the train, which was to take the team on the twelve-mile trip from Waverly to Clarksville, arrived at the Waverly station four hours late!

Sadly, competitive women's basketball in Waverly did not survive the 1920s. By the end of the decade, women students were petitioning for its revival. What they got instead was a "Girls' Athletic Association," which promoted not only on-campus programs in field hockey and basketball but the college pageant as well.

In Clinton, the story was much the same. Competitive women's basketball followed the introduction of coeducation by a year (1929), but soon it withered and died. By the time the Clinton campus was closed in 1935, women students were limited to basketball on an intra-mural basis and to a field hockey program, which played a single game against a local high school.

Lydia Wimmer
organized a women's basketball team in 1923.

In respect to [basketball players] who skipped classes on days when a game was scheduled, it was suggested that the coach be notified that such players would not be considered eligible to participate in the game.

Wartburg Normal College Faculty Council (1931)

For male students, athletic success during the years of two Wartburgs (until 1933) was often a function of scheduling. That the Wartburg Normal football team in 1923 should be able to defeat a junior high team in Waterloo by a score of 40-0 was not at all surprising. Similarly, a lopsided defeat that same year at the hands of a team from nearby Nashua could be explained by the fact that the Wartburg team was "inexperienced and light" while the opponents were experienced and averaged "at least one hundred and sixty pounds" in weight! When Wartburg in Clinton reintroduced football in 1929, it scheduled only collegiate-level competition. Not only did the team fail to win; it managed to score only a single touchdown during the entire season. Five years later, as a member of the Tri-State Conference, it shared the conference title in football (even while losing a non-conference game to the University of Dubuque by a score of 85-6). In basketball both Wartburgs competed credibly against other colleges; the Wartburg Normal Team went through the 1929 season with only a single loss—and that in the state junior college tournament.

This kind of success was one of the fruits of the increasing institutionalization of athletics during the 1920s at both Waverly and Clinton. The colleges assumed financial responsibility and began assigning faculty members to direct athletics and to serve as coaches. Except in brand-new programs, competition became almost exclusively intercollegiate. Institutional identity resulted also in the adoption of nicknames for male teams: "Spartans" in Waverly and "Knights" in Clinton.

The closing of Clinton and St. Paul-Luther in 1935 in favor of a Wartburg in Waverly inaugurated a new era in Wartburg athletics. Not everything, of course, was new. The name "Knights" and the choice of orange and black as school colors came from Clinton. So also did athletic director and "coach of everything" Elmer Hertel. Despite inadequate facilities and equipment, he managed to put into place solid programs in football, basketball, baseball, track, and tennis. In its first year, the basketball team tied for the Tri-State Conference

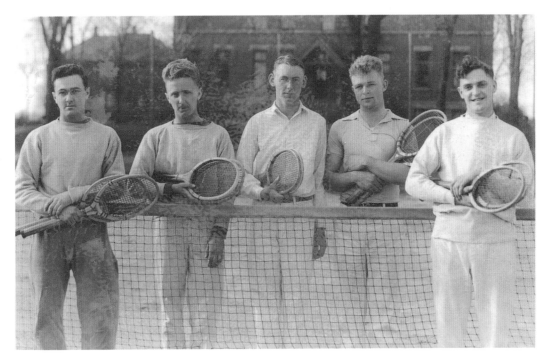

Tennis in Clinton, 1934

Elmer Hertel served as athletic director and "coach of every-thing," first at Clinton, and then in Waverly. He was also one of Wartburg's great teachers and chaired the biology department for many years.

were truncated. In 1943 football was not played at all; the following year the Iowa Conference awarded no conference championships.

The end of the war, and the return of the veterans, reinvigorated athletics at Wartburg—and almost everywhere else. Wartburg's first Iowa Conference championship came in the spring of 1947, when a self-coached team earned a share of the title in tennis. The first sustained success in athletics began a year later, when the Knights claimed the first of four consecutive Iowa Conference championships in wrestling. When Wartburg won its first conference title in basketball in 1952, it was not only the beginning of a great tradition but a powerful affirmation of the student-athlete as well. The entire starting five was on the dean's list.

Coach Axel Bundgaard followed up this centennial year success with three more basketball championships and four consecutive appearances in NCAA playoffs. The football team, winning seventeen consecutive conference games, contributed a pair of titles in 1958 and 1959; and in the early 1960s, Coach Earnest Oppermann's baseball team topped the Iowa Conference for three consecutive years. A once modest athletic program was now cranking out championships on a regular basis; postseason NCAA and NAIA appearances meant regional and even national recognition.

And there was more to come. Under Lewis "Buzz" Levick, Wartburg won fourteen Iowa Conference basketball titles, including nine in succession from 1967 through 1975. John Kurtt developed a strong program in cross country, winning three conference championships in the 1960s. Don Canfield did the same with football in the early 80s. In the mid-1970s, wrestling began another successful run under the leadership of

If you don't think you will have much—how about us? 75 boys in school and mostly 4F and pre-theological. But we will play anyway.

Elmer Hertel (1943), writing to another Iowa Conference coach

title with a record of 12 and 3. A few months later Wartburg secured much-desired admission to membership in the Iowa Intercollegiate Athletic Conference.

In all of this there was nothing much for women students except a Women's Athletic Association (WAA) to promote interest in athletics and sponsor a variety of campus competitions. Under the auspices of the WAA, a women's "varsity" team, dubbed the "Wartburg Knighties," was organized; it managed to schedule a few basketball games with area high schools. In subsequent years, WAA excursions sometimes took participants to women's "play days" and "sports days" at other colleges and universities, and occasionally into competition against a collegiate opponent.

The onset of World War II dealt a serious blow to Wartburg's drive toward competitiveness in the Iowa Conference. Male students enlisted by the scores or were drafted into the armed forces. Some pre-theological students hurried off to seminary. Travel was restricted. Sports seasons

Lewis "Buzz" Levick coached the men's basketball team to fourteen Iowa Conference titles.

Richard Walker. Following Walker's untimely death, Jim Miller brought the program to unprecedented heights in the 1990s, winning not only ten consecutive conference championships, but two NCAA Division III national titles as well.

Wartburg women finally got in on the act in the 1970s, when the college agreed to their participation in intercollegiate athletics. Gender equity was by no means instantaneous, but a solid commitment to equal emphasis on men's and women's sports rapidly took hold. Women athletes proved to be competitive from the outset. Securing an Iowa Conference championship—the first came in basketball—had to wait until 1990.

Since 1947, Wartburg Knights have won nearly 100 Iowa Conference championships—in most of the nineteen sports in which they now compete. Nearly half of the titles have come since 1990— and have been almost equally divided between men's and women's sports. In addition to the spectacular success in wrestling already noted, coaches Steve Johnson and Marcus Newsom have coached men's and women's cross country and track teams to a total of twenty-one conference championships. Under Monica Severson, the women's basketball team has finished first or second in the Iowa Conference nearly every year.

1952 Iowa Conference Championship basketball team: T. Fritschel, Bomhoff, Kurtt, Lenguadoro, Rubenow, P. Olson, Bostrack, W. Adix, Campbell, T. Olson, Engelbrecht, Bundgaard

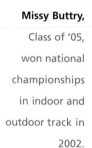

Missy Buttry,
Class of '05,
won national
championships
in indoor and
outdoor track in
2002.

men's Iowa Conference all-sports trophy five consecutive years, the women's on two occasions. Since 1970, the college has produced more than fifty academic all-Americans.

Clearly this kind of success—both athletic and academic—did not happen by accident. It is in part the result of a "long obedience in the same direction." Every president of the college since World War II has taken steps to encourage and strengthen athletics. Alumni and the Waverly community have been highly supportive. Athletic directors—Elmer Hertel, John Kurtt, Gary Grace— and a host of coaches have insisted on the kinds of excellence that honor character and integrity. Coaches have become recruiters of increasing numbers of Wartburg students; one-third of the student body now participates in intercollegiate athletics. And faculty—despite perennial worries about overemphasizing athletics—have been supportive of a program which insists that skilled athletes are first of all students, and which continues to help prepare them for lives of leadership and service.

(left) The Knights
face perennial
rival Luther on the
basketball court.

The same has been true of Wartburg football under Rick Willis. Joel Holst coached the baseball team to five consecutive championships. In other sports, success was only a little less obvious. Beginning in the mid-1990s, Wartburg won the

National Champions
Wrestlers, coaches,
and the college
president celebrated
Wartburg's first
national athletic
championship at
the 1996 NCAA
Division III wrestling
tournament:
(left to right) Alesch,
Williams, Rhodes,
S. Walker, Smith,
T. Hogan, Miller,
Fox, P. Hogan,
Halsor, Roberts,
Vogel, M. Walker,
Gerbracht, Essex

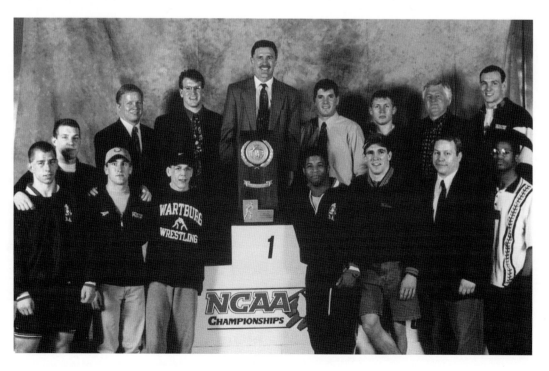